Strangely Warmed

Andrew Rumsey

Strangely Warmed

Reflections on God, Life and Bric-à-Brac

mowbray

Published by Mowbray, an imprint of the Continuum International Publishing Group

The Tower Building	80 Maiden Lane
11 York Road	Suite 704
London	New York
SE1 7NX	NY 10038

www.continuumbooks.com

The extract from 'A Letter to John Donne', is taken from C. H. Sisson, *The Trojan Ditch* (1974) and appears courtesy of Carcanet Press Limited.

First published 2010

British Library Cataloguing-in-Publication Data
A catalogue record for this book is available from the British Library.

ISBN 978-1-44113-068-6 (Paperback)

Library of Congress Cataloging-in-Publication Data
A catalog record for this book is available from the Library of Congress.

Designed and typeset by Free Range Book Design & Production Limited

Printed and bound in Great Britain by the MPG Books Group, Bodmin and King's Lynn

For Rebecca,
with love

Contents

Introduction

Scratching in his journal for May 1738, John Wesley records an evening event in London's Aldersgate Street, to which he had gone 'very unwillingly', that had, nevertheless, brought home to him a new and distinctly personal Christian faith. Describing the change that came over him 'about a quarter before nine', he writes: 'I felt my heart strangely warmed.'

Wesley chose his words well, for encounters with God down the ages seem to combine oddness and mystery with a kind of earthy closeness you would have to call local. Where, in the Old Testament, people had this kind of experience, they usually named the place after it.

This short book has emerged from the conviction that God is discovered locally: not least in the local church, where strangeness and warmth are found in equal measure. It is for those within the Church who may, just occasionally, struggle with its barminess, and also for those on the outside who are intrigued by faith but always find it beyond them.

The varied pieces contained here aren't sermons, but wholly personal reflections on Christian life, which are meant to be read a bit at a time. Someone once said that clergy are best spread thinly, like manure: you may find that the same principle applies here.

Designed for reading during Lent, the chapters loosely follow the course of that season, though in a deliberately non-programmatic fashion. Some are meant to be pondered seriously, while others simply serve to send up the worthy – that is, clergy like me. This means that you will be hard pressed to use *Strangely Warmed* as the basis for a Lenten study course – though if you do manage it, I would love to hear from you.

Christian satire has not exactly taken off as a literary genre, whereas the need for it remains as urgent as ever. The great G. K. Chesterton suggested that angels could fly because they took themselves lightly. He also knew that matters of life and death were too important not to be laughed about. If there is any single impetus for this book, it is the aspiration to lift a first foot off the ground towards his genius.

Gipsy Hill, August 2009

1. The lion's share

Attempting to cadge crisps from schoolfriends in the playground, I learned that there were, essentially, three types of person. First were those who, on offering the bag, gripped its neck so tightly around your probing fingers that – and I suspect this was the point – a greasy fragment or two was all you could extract. The second type would clasp the bag to their breast and make a great gesture of picking the particular crisp they deigned to bestow (not often one of the larger ones) before handing it over like Maundy Money to the poor. The third type – exceedingly rare in my experience – left the mouth of the bag generously open and invited you to take whichever, and however many, crisps you would like. It must be added that there were plenty who, bruised by experience, started out as the last type and ended up as the first.

Whatever our method, the fat of the land is traditionally given up at the start of Lent, having been polished off as pancakes the night before. The season of abstinence is thus bookended with banquets, which is highly symbolic. For only the worldly can become godly. It is mortals who sport the ash-smudge of Lent and sinners that are summoned to repentance. Just as those who properly adore chocolate are the only ones who may truly, if grudgingly, let it go, you cannot die to the world when you have never really lived to it, for the simple reason that it is impossible to relinquish something you don't possess.

It is significant that fasting has become Lent's vestigial limb in modern times, a residual hunger pang that remains unsated for all our vast consumption. Fasting is for feasters and Easter will be only a tantalizing taste of the new creation to those who had an appetite for the old one, and who despaired as it was finished off.

Those who really love the world must die to the world: this is the one lesson to learn in Lent. Those who are moved by the world as waves by the moon; who swoon at its beauty and rage like a jealous dad at its madness; those who, like the Psalmist, plead for their darling life to be freed from the lions: these are the ones who must surrender all. For the only means of gaining our life is to give it away.

Those who don't love the world – and there are many Christians who appear not to – really needn't worry about sacrificing it, for it is not theirs to give. They would do better to start at the beginning and receive the world on a plate. The believer who hates this world may find Christ's call to another one immensely attractive, appearing as it does to confirm their existing suspicions. But I'm not sure they will be able to follow Christ to the cross. For only those who have counted the cost of losing the world as dearly as losing a loved one are fit to follow him there. The cross of Christ will mean nothing to the unworldly, just as it meant nothing to the type of religious people who put him there. For the unworldly, death is nothing at all.

This is why, in the Gospels, the Lord loved the rich young man – not because he made a fist of seeking righteousness, but because the poor fool loved the world. And the Lord could tell that the young man loved the world so much he would never be able to let it go. He would squeeze the life out of it. The young man's dilemma is the plight of humankind and made him a prime target for the passion of Christ.

Recalling his youth, St Augustine cries to the Almighty, 'I fell upon the lovely things of your creation. You were with me but I was not with you. The beautiful things of this world kept me far from you and yet, if they had not been in you they would have had no being at all.' Having found his idolatry slowly suffocating him, the beauty of God – 'ever ancient, ever new' – blew new life into him: 'I drew breath', he confesses, 'and now I pant for you.'

The call to discipleship is a rescue for the worldly, who have the right map, as it were, but are trying to read it upside down. Turning it round replaces God as the primary object of our desire and makes everything else what Dietrich Bonhoeffer called 'penultimate'. For things to be penultimate doesn't mean they are not beautiful and glorious; it just means that they aren't, ultimately, as beautiful and glorious as God. Put positively, if we seek first the Kingdom of God, then, by their demotion, the other things added unto us gain their true status as gifts, in much the same way that the fountain pen given by my wife is more precious than any I bought for myself. In the economy of salvation, silver is gold.

The trouble is that Jesus' challenge to turn things on their head appears virtually impossible to do. In Matthew's Gospel, Jesus recruits his men as if to the Foreign Legion: no foxhole for them at night; no kitbag – just a rough cross; discomfort and persecution are to be expected and all family ties must be entirely loosened. 'Those who find their life will lose it', he says, 'and those who lose their life for my sake will find it.' You are left wondering that he even found twelve to take up the offer.

But these words aren't spoken out of nothing; like Lent, they are flanked by all that came before and after. From a God's-eye view, what went before appears to go something like this:

1. This is, by and large, a very good world. You will love it.
2. Ah, you love it rather too much. Careful now.
3. Now you've torn it. Give it back to me.
4. I said give it back, *give ... it ... back.*
5. What did I say?
6. Don't make me come down there.

Not an in-depth analysis of the Old Testament, admittedly, but it gives the gist. All that proceeds from the crux of Christ commences on Easter Sunday, with its promise of a new creation.

Relinquishing the old one, which Jesus calls all disciples to, is the crucial stage on the way to living what he termed eternal, or abundant, life. And it asks us to prise our cauterizing fingers from all the vain things that charm us most, and submit them to God, the giver. Who doesn't grip the bag, but, with an open hand, freely offers it back.

2. The other end of the telescope

The start of Lent, and still plenty of Yuletide debris to be seen down the street. Several browning brushes of Christmas trees scrub about in alleys and scraps of inflatable reindeer sag and flap from the odd drainpipe. February is a cheerless month, undecorated but for such remnants.

Among the festive clutter I'd be glad to leave in the wheelie bin, but which keeps hanging around, is the unwanted gift of the 'power ballad'. Cod-spiritual tunes that sneak in under the snowy hem of Santa's garment, power ballads pop up again throughout the year as the unavoidable accompaniment to meaningful occasions – and usually succeed in milking any such meaning dry. Lyrically, by far the most heinous of these is a song called 'From a Distance', popularized by formidable foghorn Bette Midler.

The thrust of the song is the myopic observation that, viewed from afar, all our problems and divisions are smaller and, furthermore, that 'God is watching us from a distance'. As such it reprises the folksy theme of the 1970s hit 'Melting Pot', which envisaged a kind of grim cultural apocalypse where all of our differences would be boiled away like impurities in pig-iron.

These dark sentiments may have their heart in the right place, but, alas, their eyes are dim. For a start, there is the obvious fact that, whatever God's perspective may be, we do not see our lives from a distance, but in fearful and wonderful close-up. Our peculiar detail and difference are what make us human: melt them away or blur them by distance and we cease to be. As every infant poet knows, the people may look like ants from up high, but they are not actually ants. And if we are surveyed on a green hill far away by an aloof God – a whiskery general well behind the front line – then count me as one of his conscientious objectors.

The belief in a remote deity, known as Deism, emerged during the Enlightenment of the seventeenth and eighteenth centuries, essentially to allow for the growing faith in human rationality. There being no room for him in the Inn of Reason, God – eternally accommodating – was agreed to have withdrawn to a kind of divine potting shed at the bottom of the garden, leaving the young ones to their clever arguments. Philosophy hadn't buried God yet, just moved him into a granny flat.

To imagine that God is thus semi-detached is, I suppose, one way to cope with the troubles of a world which the Almighty may not appear to do anything about. It's the way plenty chose amidst the unbearable wave of grief that overtook the British people after 1918, when folk religion offered a powerful anaesthetic, removing both God and man from the horrific reality. Canon Scott-Holland's desperately popular poem, 'Death is nothing at all', applies the ether perfectly.

As an outlook, though, it makes for a bleak midwinter. Yet despite being pretty much the polar opposite of the gospel message, it is surprising how often a kind of Deism appears in everyday Christianity – due in part to theologians having quaffed large lungfuls of Platonism in the first centuries after Christ.

Platonic thought tended to keep anything eternal (truth, beauty, disputes with the Inland Revenue, etc.) at arm's length from the material world and the Church has never quite succeeded in bridging the divide. In order to point my howitzers directly at this tendency, here is a light and radio-friendly Thought for the Day, which might be served up on the airwaves just as Ms Midler is mercifully faded down …

Hello. A wise man once said, 'If you want to give God a laugh, tell him your plans.' I like to think it is the same when we tell him of our troubles.

You see, to us, the problems of life seem immense, but we forget that this isn't how they appear to God. To God, they are no problem! We spend so much of our time painfully aware of our concerns, but rarely do we remember that they aren't a concern for him. And by simply learning to see things from God's perspective, it's amazing how much smaller our problems become.

Imagine this a bit like a telescope: look through it the usual way and everything seems much closer and more threatening than it really is. But if you just look through the other end, suddenly it all shrinks down to size! Perhaps, later on today, you might try this for real: find an old telescope or pair of binoculars and walk around for an hour or two looking through the other end. What a difference this will make to everyday experiences like eating or crossing the road – things won't loom quite so large, then!

Most of us long just to forget our worries for a while. My friends, thankfully God has done this for us. Think for a minute: we can be completely mistaken, but not God; we can be utterly bewildered, but not

God; we can be greatly bothered – but not God. He cannot be bothered in the least.

You know, God has a great sense of humour. I often imagine how amused he must be by our silly little schemes and muddles. Take a moment to imagine God laughing at your struggles, putting them all into proportion. How does that make you feel? It's particularly effective to do when things get too much and we are at our lowest ebb. In the silent solitude of your bedroom tonight, why not bring to mind whatever troubles you most and, if helpful, picture God laughing about it – not just with an indulgent smile, but really laughing himself silly at all you have to cope with. Doesn't that put a different complexion on it?

In pastoral ministry I have always endeavoured to take people's heavy burdens and *make light of them*. It is immensely rewarding to see the effect – sometimes quite visibly – on people's faces as I nod, smile and chuckle gently at this or that personal crisis. For whatever is a crisis for them certainly isn't for God. It may be their problem, but it is not his problem – or mine! *Do you see?* So, next time you fall flat on your face, try to see yourself as God must: not from under a puddle! But from a distance.

3. The last enemy to be destroyed is bric-a-brac

We have just had a bric-a-brac sale at church. In these murky areas of religion, it is vital to define one's terms. Bric-a-brac, in the unerring words of Harry in my congregation, is 'hard jumble', and after the locusts have gone, we still have six creaking trestles of the stuff.

Surveying the wondrous dross this afternoon, perhaps I can tempt you with a china kitten, lifting its paw in a pleading posture? Or maybe a wobbly mug tree, or some rose-shaped tea lights, or a pair of comedy antlers? No? Then how about a frankly unsettling model scarecrow stuffed with raffia, or more dried flowers than you could shake a dried stick at? Be my guest. Please.

Human beings, the Book of Genesis tells us, are made in the image of God: they are distinguished from other creatures in significant ways. Some point to our senses of wonder or humour as marks of this difference; others to our capacity for reflection or rational thought. Personally, I am clear that what sets us apart from the apes is bric-a-brac: our capacity to create it, collect it, and still have twelve baskets of it left after all else has been consumed. Scuttle aside, O cockroach; lay low, ye ancient hills of disposable nappies, for bric-a-brac will outlast you all.

A bric-a-brac sale captures the human condition in a nutshell – actually in a porcelain nutshell surmounted by a rustic fisherman. It is truly remarkable how we imitate creation by reproducing it in microform, and then fetishize what we have made. Even in ages and cultures not so bulimically gorged with stuff as our own, bric-a-brac persists, with toys and ornaments emerging from old cans or scraps of soap. We are instinctively artistic, even if most of our art lacks a certain divine spark. Extracting a rib from Adam's prone form, the Lord fashioned the fathomless beauty of womankind. You can bet that Adam, presented with the same rib, would have whittled it into a pipe rack.

Human aptitude for creating things may positively reflect our status as creatures, but, as the second Adam observed, this knack for hoarding up our little treasures is a fatal crack in our clay – self-centred and only bound for decay. Hell could well be a closing-down sale where wailing shoppers tussle over trinkets, as if their deaths depended on it.

If it lies anywhere, salvation is in releasing our sweaty grip, and saying 'after you'. This is what George Steiner calls the *courtesy* of true art, which doesn't seek to grab, smother and possess, but stands back to make space, regardless of personal cost.

You can do this at a bric-a-brac sale, of course, although it won't raise much money for the new church hall. But then bric-a-brac is already inherently cheap – that's part of its appeal. Driving recently through a small town in North Wales, I passed one of those fearful shops selling 'fancy goods'. As I waited at the lights, my blood quietly curdling, I noticed that we were being enticed inside by a pile of opaque plastic bags, all tied at the top. Above them was a sign which read 'bags of bric-a-brac, 50p'.

The idea that you might pop out for a random assortment of bric – or indeed brac – without knowing what was in it, struck me as truly priceless.

Perhaps curiosity is to blame. In Greek mythology, Pandora is given an interesting bit of hard jumble by Zeus: a box (no doubt made out of clothes pegs by Zeus's dad), which he forbade her ever to open. Having been to numerous bring-and-buy sales, though, Pandora naturally wanted to peek inside to see if the box contained some other pleasing trifle – a jigsaw, perhaps. When she did so, we are told that the evils of humankind – plague, sorrow, poverty, crime (and, I hazard, the intemperate love of fancy goods) burst out upon the world, though she shut it just in time to preserve one last quality, hope. Learning her lesson, Pandora quickly passed the box on to her local Cancer Research.

The ballooning business of charity shopping to a certain extent redeems our crazy craving by offering a guilt-free path to self-indulgence. But when Sue Ryder or the Cats' Protection League own every other shop on your high street, two things at least are clear: first that the ground rents are too high and second, that we all have far too much stuff.

In the limitless tide of unwanted flotsam that swills and spills between these emporia, there is a kind of food chain. If one was especially perverse, one could map the progress of an item of bric-a-brac – say a Charley Pride album or a commemorative teaspoon – and find the point at which it was successfully scavenged, found a home or finally entered the landfill.

Which is probably where we will pay the true price for our inconspicuous consumption. Until then, though, we all love a bargain.

4. The mild man of Borneo

Bishop Howes

One of the more rewarding experiences in church life lately has been to attend a 'self-defence for softies' class, run for clergy in this neck of the woods. Obviously there were good, commonsense reasons for doing this (a few minor scuffles during after-church coffee, nothing too serious) but I also went along because the comic potential of such an occasion promised to be limitless. Surely watching some of the mildest-mannered people on God's earth, collars askew, grappling with one another, would be too good to miss. Happily I was not disappointed.

The highlight of the day arrived when our trainer, Steve, tried in vain to persuade the least assertive person I have ever encountered to 'come at him' with an attacking blow. He might as well have asked her to walk on the ceiling, for here was a woman of quite phenomenal meekness, one for whom – as I inadvertently glimpsed whilst changing – lowliness had indeed become her inner clothing.

In an episode evocative of Balaam and his Ass, Steve coaxed and provoked her – even deliberately spilling her cup of Mellow Bird's – all to no avail. She may have been seething beneath the surface, but it just didn't connect to her limbs until, at what must have been the apex of her fury, she unleashed a strange, stroking movement that, had he been a greenfly, might have caused a moment's irritation, but, as he was not, merely served to smooth out the creases on his tracksuit.

Rare fun. Reflecting on this since, it strikes me that Western Christians nowadays might be lacking a certain vigour when it comes to working out their faith. This is perfectly evoked in one of Garrison Keillor's Lake Woebegone stories about a group of Lutheran pastors on a boat trip, which concludes with the wonderful scene of the boat slowly sinking into the lake and 'twenty four ministers standing up to their smiles in water, chins up, trying to understand this experience and its deeper meaning'.

Clergy in particular can tend to be those for whom strength of feeling is explored rather than enacted, and nowhere is this more apparent than in the way we speak – usually with a curious sort of italicized *emphasis* on things that are particularly *meaningful*. This can be a useful habit to pick up, suggesting as it does that you are a bit like Wordsworth when he writes, 'To me the meanest flower that blows can give thoughts that do often lie too deep for tears.'

My feeling is that we overdo this a little. Soon after the self-defence shenanigans, I attended another meeting at which the facilitator asked us to share the *joys* and *sorrows* (that's pros and cons to the rest of you) of having a curate in training. While I struggled to mine the deep seams of emotion that were clearly expected, one of my neighbours responded by describing the *sheer joy* of watching their colleague's emergent vocation, at which everyone around the room nodded sagely and gave the occasional 'mmmm'. I mean, really.

Perhaps what we need is a revival of Muscular Christianity, the nineteenth-century movement that, through novelists such as Charles Kingsley and Thomas Hughes, espoused masculine heroes and the spiritual benefits of robust physical exercise. According to Kingsley and Hughes, the Church had gone soft. It needed to show some backbone and get some fresh air. It needed, in other words, a blast of the pastoral care given by The Almighty to poor, sickly Job, who, after 36 chapters of wound-licking, receives God's soothing solution: 'GIRD UP YOUR LOINS LIKE A MAN'.

Whatever its undoubted shortcomings, this era certainly produced characters of remarkable discipline and perseverance, often in the mission field. I recently came across an obituary in the *Church Times* for the late Bishop of Kuching (which sounds like a wealthy diocese), the Rt Revd Peter Howes, who spent most of his 92 years working alone as a missionary in Borneo.

Among his exploits, this human dynamo translated the New Testament into the local Dayak language whilst imprisoned by the Japanese, writing on the backs of labels from cans and hiding the texts under the floorboards of his hut; he survived tropical ulcers by plunging headlong into a riverbed of slimy black mud and worked a mind-boggling 140-hour week in his jungle 'parish' until well into his seventies. All this from a bookish, slightly bewildered-looking parson of the sort you might meet tending his roses in Ruislip.

Taking a warm bath to recover from reading this heroic tale, I couldn't help pondering how bland and self-indulgent the obituaries of my invertebrate generation will seem in comparison. While we rest in peace, they will rise, promptly, in glory.

5. The sea is his

Jesus grafitti on Brighton West Pier

The first view of the sea should always merit a prize. On family excursions to the coast it meant the end was in sight – for our asthmatic Austin Maxi, her exhausted driver and unravelling passengers. Addled and saddlesore, you couldn't always be certain; that grey-green wash on the horizon might be sky or a line of far hills – possibly it was a mirage induced by fumes from the Maxi's scorching vinyl seats. But turn another corner or crest a slope and the ocean rolled out before you: undeniable, overwhelming.

The sea marks the terminus of our control, and this too brings relief. As the road approaches the beach and signs reach left or right – but not ahead – you can begin to relax, as to take a coastal route is to beat the bounds of your territory. Such paths mark out both possession and non-possession. Travelling them should bring a meekness which enables you to inherit the earth.

From Eden and childhood we are fascinated by the lines drawn between safety and danger; permission and transgression; mine and not-mine. This makes the coast the most natural place in the world to play, to dance in and out of the waves: *they've got me – no they haven't!* The tide is a mesmerizing threshold between worlds; piers are merely a kind of forgivable trespass, a sandcastle game that pretends to extend into a domain which can never be ours. This is why their inevitable destruction by the sea is so poignant; their rusted stumps and stranded arcades so transfixing and oddly terrifying. '*Get them back in*,' you want to cry, extending your arms like a harbour.

The terrible playfulness of the sea is a primal theme in our imagination. In the wisdom and poetry books of the Bible it becomes a motif for all that surges beyond our comprehension, 'wherein are things creeping innumerable' – chief among them being Leviathan, the monstrous serpent who frolics amidst chaos.

In the book of Job, the vastness and mystery of the sea is presented in response to Job's wretched appeal for answers in the face of his torment. 'Where were you when I laid the foundations of the earth?' thunders The Almighty. 'Tell me, if you have understanding.'

Who shut in the sea with doors, when it burst out from the womb? When I made the cloud its garment, and thick darkness its swaddling band, and prescribed bounds for it, and set bars and doors, and said, thus far you shall come, and no farther: and here shall your proud waves be stopped?

This is a backdrop to human suffering, not an explanation of its detail. Job is in a slippery place, which he is no more able to fathom than he is to keep Leviathan as a pet goldfish. 'Will you play with it as with a bird', asks God, with plunging irony, 'or will you put it on a leash for your girls?'

Such context and perspective, like the sea itself, is both dreadful and reassuring. To accept, for example, that a maelstrom of subconscious thought churns beneath the conscious mind mildly selecting its holiday over a tranquil glass of wine is a disturbing notion. When our dreams bubble this madness to the surface we duck them back down again pretty sharply. And yet God's background to Job's condition also buoys us up, because it proclaims, like the Psalmist, that 'the sea is his and he made it'. The depths are sounded and bounded by their creator, we read. Thus far you shall come, and no farther.

The biblical narrative suggests that chaos is not our final destination. In the prophecy of Isaiah, Leviathan ('that crooked serpent') is slain as an indication of God's rescue plan for his people. Crucially, in the bookending vision of Revelation, St John sees 'a new heaven and a new earth: for the first heaven and the first earth were passed away; and there was no more sea'. A River of Life, curiously, but no sea.

Perhaps the most compelling sign of God's mastery over the deep comes in those Gospel chapters where Jesus appears, after midnight, walking upon the water; or waking from unruffled sleep in the squall-tossed trawler to order the waves 'Peace, be still.'

Jesus walking on the water is a dreamlike image, and one with a tenacious hold on our folk memory. Even though usually cited to disparage the credulity of believers, we picture him still, and no doubt will as long as we are adrift.

Matthew portrays a ghostly figure, which petrified rather than comforted those disciples being buffeted by the storm. Famously, it is Peter alone who, with typical rashness, climbs overboard and starts to walk towards his Lord. Not unlike a cartoon character who continues to run off the edge of a cliff until he realizes there is nothing beneath him, he then begins to sink, immediately caught by Jesus, with whom he gets back into the boat.

Over the years, I have heard or given several dozen sermons on this passage. It strikes me that, when posing the perennial question – ideally over one's spectacles – 'and *why* did Peter sink?', none of these homilies has ever given or expected the most natural reply of all, namely: 'He sank *because he was in the water.*'

As Jesus chides Peter for his lack of faith, it feels like a similar shortfall on our part to state the obvious. But I'm not sure it is. In Matthew's account, Peter asked for what he got: Jesus didn't say 'come' until Peter had requested him to – needing proof that it really was Jesus and not a phantom. The Lord's initial command to those quaking in their boats was simply to take courage and not be afraid. The apostle's want of faith stems from his disbelief that the apparition could be Christ himself: that the sea was his.

Interestingly, one of the earliest and most common artistic depictions of the Christian Church was a small vessel bobbing on the water. It was a good emblem for the time: the little fellowship braving the waves of horrific persecution. But it could well apply in any age, given that faith is the only way to cross the place where everyone is out of their depth.

Seaside memories are, for me, littered with near-death experiences. My late father was a responsible, level-headed sort of man in most contexts. He wore driving gloves and piloted an Austin Maxi. But with the first draughts of sea air, he inhaled an untamed recklessness into his soul. On one holiday to Devon in the mid-1970s he hired a small rowing boat and took his three sons out into a very dangerous estuary, ignoring all warnings that the tide was going out and we would likely become stranded on a sandbank. *Nonsense*, said my father, until the tide went out and we became stranded on a sandbank.

Far from land, and with evening drawing in, our options were somewhat limited. So, in a slightly more self-preserving version of the Peter incident, he ordered my eldest brother, who was blessed with a pair of extraordinarily long legs, to jump out of the boat and walk back to shore in order to fetch help.

With hindsight, had he been a couple of years older, he would probably have said 'No Dad, I will surely sink'. But we were still – just – at the age when we simply did what he told us to, even if it seemed like lunacy. So, my brother negotiated his legs over the side and I can see him now, thigh deep in mud, wading like a curlew across the bay.

He made it, I should add. To his undying credit, he also raised the alarm and led the coastguard to retrieve my shamefaced father and his shivering disciples.

In the imagination of their hearts, Britons have more than once believed that they ruled the waves: a proud myth, destined to be scattered like a wrecked pier or a stranded dinghy. But it is nothing. The sea is his.

6. Feeling the benefit

'The English Electric Lightning, Britain's celebrated all-weather jet fighter, will sadly not be flying this afternoon, owing to the fog.' This memorable announcement, tannoyed to a Pacamac-clad crowd at the 1977 Finningley Airshow, epitomizes the subjection of the British people to their elements. It came, needless to say, on a Bank Holiday, and is as redolent of those lost Mondays as coffee from a tartan Thermos.

Shall I, then, compare thee to a summer's day? Well it rather depends, doesn't it. You see, it could be exceptionally mild for the time of year or it might have begun to turn a bit chilly. It may have been lovely when I got up, but for some reason seem to have clouded over since breakfast. But you never know, it could clear up this afternoon.

Amid the tempest of world affairs it may comfort the government to recognize that there is only one Special Relationship that really matters to the British, and it is with the weather. This is probably because we have so much of it: visit the Met Office's lavish web-shrine and you will find such phrases as 'marked seasonal variations' and 'notoriously changeable' cropping up in nearly every sentence. Our weather is a constant, close companion and its varying moods shape the way we describe our own – 'under the weather', 'a little gloomy', 'bright and breezy'.

Fittingly, the vagaries of the national climate find liturgical expression in the Anglican Book of Common Prayer, specifically in the canticle known as the Benedicite. Traditionally said at Matins, this is basically a hymn to everything in creation, especially the weather. 'O ye dews and frosts, bless ye the Lord: praise him and magnify him for ever', it runs, urging the showers, ice, snow and clouds to do the same. This, for centuries, was how thousands of our compatriots began their day. Whilst lifted from the Apocrypha, you feel it could have been penned by Michael Fish.

Given all this, it is hardly surprising to find Dr Johnson observing that, 'When two Englishmen meet, their first talk is of the weather.' However, across the kingdom the weather exists not merely as a topic, but as a mode and medium of conversation, a way of indirectly relating to one another. This extends from a cursory 'lovely day' to the postman to lengthy, often animated conversations with complete strangers about clouds and their likely contents. When, in the street recently, an unusually loud thunderclap caused everyone to start, the instant and striking effect was for us to smile at fellow pedestrians and begin to chat, as if jolted into awareness of each other's presence. Nothing else gives this immediate passport to intimacy – strike up a similar conversation about architecture, for instance, or varieties of butterfly, and you will find people edging away from you uneasily at bus stops.

This subtle social contract means that, when the weather turns against us during, say, Wimbledon, we are not so much frustrated as hurt that it isn't playing the game. The Great Storm of 1987 was Britain's worst natural disaster for 300 years, claiming at least eighteen lives and costing close to £800 million in damages. The abiding impression, though, was a sense of national betrayal – not just by the forecasters, but by the weather itself, which had so blatantly overstepped the mark.

A persistent bafflement at the richness and variety of our climate is one of our most comical national characteristics. One might have thought that centuries of sunny intervals and squally showers would have taught us barely to lift an eyebrow when the clouds darken, but it is not so. Each morning we rise with puzzled alarm at the fickleness of our weather, as if it had hitherto been a byword for predictability. Such a striking, goldfish-like tendency means that we also display a woeful lack of preparedness in dealing with it, such that the lightest dusting of snow or slightly gusty autumn day is enough to bring the country slithering to a standstill.

Hence our obsession with the weather forecast, which many Britons approach with horoscopic awe. National forecasts began when the Met Office was formed 150 years ago by Robert FitzRoy, Captain of Charles Darwin's ship the *Beagle*, to provide meteorological and sea current information to mariners. The seafaring connotations remain central to our island's romance with weather prediction, surrounded as we are by turbulent forces beyond our control. Over the gale-pitched waves of our imagining ring the mysterious incantations of the Shipping Forecast which, for transcendence, beat *Thought for the Day* by several leagues.

Addressing a crowd, possibly on a Bank Holiday, Jesus squints at the firmament and says to them, 'When you see a cloud rising in the west, you immediately say "it is going to rain"; and so it happens … You hypocrites! You know how to interpret the appearance of earth and sky, but why do you not know how to interpret the present time?' For a country which has always looked into the heavens as into a mirror, his words hit home, as we are rightly unnerved by the increasingly apocalyptic outlook for our climate.

The dread words 'since records began' are now heard with alarming frequency as global warming nudges the mercury ever higher each year. The year 1659 – when national temperatures began to be officially recorded – marks the barometer-tapper's Anno Domini, but no one is quite sure where it will all end. As we peer up into an uncertain sky, the abiding question is not so much what we say about the weather, but what it says about us.

7. The rucksack theory

A friend was on a hiking holiday in the English Lake District. During an especially arduous climb, one of her party began to flag and lag behind the group so, silencing the rhythmic swish of Gore-Tex, they all decided to rest for a moment and snap open some Kendal Mint Cake. Addressing their exhausted companion, another advised, 'One of us should give you their rucksack to carry as well.' When the hollow laughter subsided, she persisted, 'No, I'm serious – it's true. If you're tired out on a walk, that's what you do – carry an extra rucksack and you'll begin to feel better.' Then came the clincher: 'It's what my mum and dad always told me.'

She was entirely in earnest: well into her twenties the poor chump believed that doubling your load would, against all logic and common sense – let alone weary experience – somehow reduce the overall burden and enable you to skip from crag to crag like a mountain goat. Just imagine her smirking parents, springing along nimbly in front of their wheezing children who, bent double with Gaz stoves and groundsheets, press on, oblivious to the deceit. Picture them uncorking their glee over the dinner table – *You'll never guess what we told our lot ... yep ... swallowed every word ... that's right, totally wore them out ...* One hardly dares wonder whether they could resist extending the principle to other areas of their daughter's life – *Not happy tidying your room, love? Better do the whole house and you'll feel much better ...* Part of you wants to strap them to a hundredweight pack and deposit them on Dartmoor: the other part wants to buy them a drink.

This – pleasingly true – story shows not only how fiendish parents can be, but also how completely children bear the impression of those whom they trust. Smacked or smothered, a child will assume their experience is normal: this is childhood's resilience and its utter vulnerability. Gradually, through comparison with others, we grow aware that not everyone, say, dances round maypoles or says grace before Sunday lunch, but such things remain normative for us, long into the future. Whether or not you encumber your children with camping gear, they will, I'm afraid, always be carrying your baggage.

This has to be acknowledged in any conversation about the 'indoctrination' of children in matters of religion. It is a commonplace to assert that – especially at school, but also at home – children must not be influenced in any decision they make about God. In a pluralist society religious truth-claims tend to be quarantined, placed in a vacuum, and viewed as such an infectious virus that they can only be safely handled under laboratory conditions. In this most contingent and communal area of life, children must be left 'free to choose'.

But, in an important sense, a child is no freer to choose God than they are to choose their own parents. The truth of life begins with its givenness, which the Christian knows as Grace. Before we can apprehend it, life is bestowed on us: we don't seek to be born, we just are. And the child soon finds a whole bunch of other things have been handed down, too – her mother's attractive neighing laugh, her sister's dungarees, her father's rucksack.

A huge proportion of the influences upon us – accidents of time, place and culture – are simply given – and this doesn't let up in adulthood. However clinically a teacher handles a topic – religious or otherwise – they will inevitably be indoctrinating their pupils. All you can hope is that the yoke of their teaching will be easy and the burden light.

Knowledge of the truth, like freedom, is a function of relationship and nobody, unless they happen to live on the moon, is free from the social conditioning this involves. Indeed, the few unfortunates who are denied society aren't free at all but usually imprisoned or insane. The irony is that, as the Scottish philosopher John Macmurray affirmed, we discover selfhood and individuality only insofar as we relate to that which is not ourselves. Beginning with the reciprocal love of mother and child, personal identity is formed in learning the correspondence between 'I' and 'Thou' – the dance in which we approach and withdraw from those with whom we are bound to move through life.

Whenever one partner dominates that dance, there is the need to reassert our own freedom of expression. Against the bloody background of the French religious wars, René Descartes coined his famous dictum 'I think, therefore I am.' This was a sharp stamp on the foot of received truth, but to a certain extent it left us dancing on our own, like dads at a wedding reception – bowing to no one in the novelty of our moves and caught up in the fantasy of our brilliance.

For Descartes, the only trustworthy home for truth was inside your own head – there could be no real touching point between mind and matter, no slow smooch between the subjective thinker and the object of his desire. This split, so influential for the way we think today, was robustly chaperoned by the towering doorman of the Enlightenment, Immanuel Kant. We can never know something 'in itself', he argued: all we can truly know and prove are the 'phenomena' our senses perceive. Applying this rigorous entry policy, he marshalled the stuff of life into separate lists, one for facts and one for beliefs. Anyone in the queue who claimed to know ultimate truth but couldn't prove it was left in the cold. Or they could shelter in the church down the road.

Hence our reticence about the truth-claims of religion, which, to many, seem as winkingly spurious as those of our gullible hiker's parents. The problem with the apartheid between fact and belief is that most matters of fact are also articles of faith, as the philosopher of science Michael Polanyi demonstrated a generation ago. The quest for truth, he argued, was an adventure, an investigation which required placing complete trust in the tools you have – Newton's laws, for example – even if those tools turn out to be faulty. Polanyi held that we know the truth 'tacitly' as a kind of hunch, and that, as we faithfully feel our way ahead, our explorations may find the truth coming to meet us from the other side, like Stanley greeting Livingstone, or the father welcoming the prodigal.

The gap between what you believe to be true and what is actually true will usually be bridged by faith, hope or love – St Paul's trio of indestructible tools for life. The employment of one or all of these will often demonstrate whether the truth you are pursuing is real or not. If you believe in fairies, to snatch an example out of the air, then my advice is not to hold back – rest your whole weight on their gossamer wings and see if they will carry you. Build complex fairy cities; forge Tinker Bell statues for every park and frame your legal system with her precepts. Along the way, you'll begin to get a sense of whether she is there at all.

For her wholehearted belief in the lightness of her double-burden, our rambling friend is commendable, despite the enjoyable failure of her thesis when tested on wider society. She did, after all, make the most of what she was given. At the Last Supper, Jesus told his disciples, 'You did not choose me, but I chose you … to go and bear fruit – fruit that will last.' And by the fruits of our faith, our grasp of the truth will be known.

8. Into the mystic

Maybe it's the onset of Lent, or indigestion, but there are stirrings within. Such periodic growling of the soul is, in part at least, an inherited phenomenon; signalling my family's uneasy relationship with things mystical and monastic.

This is typified by an episode featuring my late father at London Bridge station sometime in the mid-1950s. Having absconded at dusk from the monastery which he had rashly entered a few months earlier – I like to think a secret tunnel was involved – he was pursued cross-country from Dorset by the abbot, confronted on the smog-laden platform and piously pressed to reconsider. 'Think of everything you can't have with us', I imagine the abbot remonstrating. 'Would you give all that up for this?' He did, I'm relieved to say. Above the same spot now hangs a massive recruitment poster, whose oily enquiry, 'Dreaming of a bigger package?', is almost enough to make me consider heading down to Dorset and picking up where Dad left off.

Withdrawal of this sort both attracts and repels us. There are certain times when a life of contemplation seems both attainable and desirable: during a hot bath, for example, or just before settling down to work. These can, I find, induce an earnest desire to empty oneself of all activity and simply *be*. There are plenty of other times, however, when the deep things of the soul seem as improbable and disquieting as those disclosed by television documentaries about the mutant and murky life of the seabed.

Possibly for this reason, the contemplative tradition, which emerged with the growth of monasticism across North Africa and Europe, is, for many believers, a vast Antarctica of the spiritual world: a void so threatening and huge that it has been kept at the margins of popular spirituality as a territory reserved for the intrepid or eccentric few.

In fairness, the mystics have not exactly discouraged such an impression. This is the tradition, remember, that brought you Simeon Stylites, the fifth-century saint who spent half his life sitting on a sixty-foot pillar (maybe as a pleasantly comfortable alternative to the pews in his local church). Such ardent battiness is quite outstanding, even for Christianity. Ever since the first Christian hermits retreated to the deserts of Egypt in the third century, many in the Church have secretly felt that this was perhaps the best place for them.

But while self-denial is always easy to lampoon, even the loopier ascetics uphold a Christian theme which is strangely alluring in these times. To shed all but our thirst for God; to leave behind the emotional and material clutter that crowds us and live in simple awareness of the gift of life: what a release that must be. Well, yes and no. As Thomas Merton wrote, 'Men do not become saints by ceasing to be men', and, far from escaping our neighbour and ourselves, in retreat our fleshly failings can become all too apparent. Monks get nasty, too, I'm afraid.

Then there is God. According to the authorities, the contemplative path is a *via negativa*, which proceeds like a pinball bouncing off everything that God is not, aware that all words and concepts about him are ultimately inadequate. What follows such a process of elimination, they say, is not blissful enlightenment, but something akin to a murky day in Basingstoke.

Dark night of the soul, cloud of unknowing – call it what they will – the mystical way is about the painful paradox of God being conspicuous by his absence; being seen in the not-seeing. An insight, you might think, destined to cheer only the chalice-is-half-empty brigade. And, possibly, Leonard Cohen.

I'm aware that I may be underselling the idea. But the shedding of all else save our desire for God is something every believer has to face eventually, and the end of contemplation is never to discard the world, simply to release things so they may be viewed aright. Human nature generally tends towards loving things to death. Contemplation dies into life.

There's really no need to shin up a pole, unless you especially want to; the everyday mystic begins by stepping back and giving fresh attention to the things that lie under their nose. To whet your appetite for a spot of reflection, sample this well-known passage from Julian of Norwich:

> He (God) showed me something small, no bigger than a hazelnut, lying in the palm of my hand, as it seemed to me, and it was as round as a ball. I looked at it with the eye of my understanding and thought: What can this be? And I was given this general answer: It is everything which is made.

At this spiritually dyspeptic time of year, such morsels of the monastery can be nourishing indeed. But no, I couldn't manage a whole one.

9. Then we'll take over the world

Darkly tanned by tannin stands 'The Wigmore' Insulated Tea Urn. Languishing in a skip, tipped-out innards stained and drained away; paint scheme cream and green like England was, a few rusty leaves remain. The spring-cleaning work party at church had unearthed it, so – along with a pair of death-trap trestles, legs snapping back like terrier's jaws, restrained by rope – I wrestled the old vessel home, half-minded to grow a thatch of geraniums from its lid.

Beholding this icon carries you to a nearly-lost vision of local life. You can hear the chink and creak of canvas-backed seats being unstacked and sat in – watch the tombola's lumping roll and scattering of Beetle-drive dice. Stare for long enough and, with a fair degree of accuracy, I suspect you would also be able to guess the weight of the cake.

The Wigmore must have saturated the parish with tea in its heyday – how many hundred scalding cups did it serve up to all and sundry? Barn dances; bring-and-share lunches; Cub Scout gang shows: manned by an army of

Pams and Margarets, a never-failing stream spewed from its spout, a well-stewed river of life flowing out through the church hall hatch and into the neighbourhood.

Finding the old urn, I felt a little as one imagines the High Priest Hilkiah felt when, in the Book of Kings, he discovered an ancient book of Mosaic law during Josiah's repairs to the temple. No doubt seizing a rare opportunity to turf out some old songbooks and thoughtfully bequeathed kneelers, Hilkiah stumbled upon what may have been the Book of Deuteronomy, which he promptly had taken and read aloud to the young king.

On hearing how far short his subjects had fallen of God's commands, Josiah organized a public reading of the book to all his people, 'both small and great', sparking in the process something of a national revival.

If a revival is likely in our own time, it could well spring from recovering a discarded tea urn, which warmly embodies the Christian law of love for neighbour. Tea is never just tea, after all: it is consolation and companionship, it is admission into society. 'I had a cup of tea', wrote George Orwell, nervously visiting a kitchen for navvies in Limehouse; 'it was a kind of baptism. After that my fears vanished.'

Every home needs a kettle, but every community needs an urn. The church was never the only tea-giver, but it was the principal one – largely because, until the 1890s, the ecclesiastical parish was the appointed source of all charity, education and poor relief in each district. Long after parliament had relieved it of this responsibility, the local church endured as the focus of common life. In some places, it still does.

The growth of cities was crucial to this shift away from the parish as the primary unit of English society, but, even in urban areas, the persistence of churches as hubs for local life is striking. Quite when their urns started to run dry is a moot point: according to the historian Callum Brown, author of *The Death of Christian Britain*, it didn't really become noticeable until the 1960s – around the time John Lennon made his famous offhand jibe about the Beatles being 'bigger than Jesus'.

With such spiritual sand kicked in its face, the Church has become ever more frantic about its size. Each successive publication of attendance statistics is read like a dreaded business account, market share graphing gloomily downwards. In such a climate, ministers may mimic Brian Epstein, chivvying their congregations with tales of 10,000-strong churches in Asia (we may not sell many records here, the inference being, but we're massive in Singapore), and pour every effort into showing that, far from fading away, *we are gonna be huge.*

But does Jesus need to be bigger than the Beatles? When asked if he was optimistic or pessimistic about the future of the Church in the West, the missionary theologian Lesslie Newbigin was fond of replying, 'Christ is Risen, so as far as I'm concerned the question doesn't arise.' What he meant was that Christianity stood or fell not on the success of an institution, but on the historical events surrounding its founder.

The resurrection is announced by scripture as *gospel* – news to be reported, not a target to be achieved. Christ sent the Church to proclaim this news to all nations, but the question remains how large it needs to be in order to fulfil that commission. Its vision is of a kingdom, not an empire – a subtlety which, it may be said with hefty understatement, Christendom never quite grasped. Empire looks to expand its own power and territory: the Kingdom of God shouldn't need to conquer the earth, for the earth – and everything in it, sings the Psalm – is already the Lord's.

Jesus often compared the Kingdom to a very small thing that has universal effect – yeast working through a batch of dough, for instance. As such, the quantity serves the quality – you need enough yeast to make the whole loaf rise, but not too much or it overflows and can fall flat.

Parish life was never just about numbers, it was about pursuing all that makes for peace and builds up our common life. Churches must recover a local imagination, of the sort where salvation began with the wangling of a welly, or where you root through a pile of musty jumble only to tug at the hem of your dreams.

Christian society can turn up some surprising rewards, after all. It was by virtue of their belonging within such a community that, at the 1957 church fete in the Liverpool parish of St Peter's, Woolton, a teenage John Lennon first bumped into Paul McCartney.

Without the local congregation, they would never have met, let alone become bigger than Jesus. So charge up The Wigmore, Margaret, and the church will brew again.

10. Quirk of art

Twenty years ago I choreographed and performed in a spoof worship dance at a well-known Christian arts festival. This was essentially a tribute to the cheesecloth-clad pioneers of praise, The Fisherfolk, from whose *oeuvre* we chose the evergreen, 'Ask and it shall be given'. The accompanying dance was, as I recall, perfectly executed: we gleefully sprang aloft in the classic 'praise fountain' style; shielding our eyes, we turned aside in men-loved-darkness-rather-than-light ignominy; and we wore crepe paper streamers on our wrists.

Having expected wry grins to greet our Gillette-like irony, to my alarm I found myself engaged in an early pastoral encounter with a young man for whom the dance had clearly touched hitherto unplumbed depths. 'That was incredibly moving,' he said.

This inability to control how others will interpret what is portrayed to them is the slippery thing about art – one man's ichthus will be another man's *poisson*, so to speak. Indeed, this hospitality of meaning is precisely what most artists enjoy about their medium.

But for Christians, who have a gospel to proclaim, it can mean the arts are viewed with suspicion. They aren't clear enough, and allow too much room for misunderstanding, for people Not Getting It. If viewed in this manner, artistic expression of faith will be kept on a short leash, employed merely to illustrate an otherwise firmly made point. Worse still, art can end up being used like those infernal emoticons that deface emails and texts, appending a punctuated wink or seething demon to each message, just to double-underline our intention.

The same spirit is more entertainingly at work in the laminated notices which transform every church kitchen into a gallery of careful instruction. Through a riot of inverted commas, the procedure for making yourself a cup of coffee will be bludgeoned upon you with all the insane emphasis of an Englishman in Spain explaining his sunburn to the chemist. These works really merit a major exhibition – a thought for Back to Church Sunday, perhaps.

The possibility of not hearing the message is present in any creative act, including the first and greatest. The poet-king David picks up this theme in Psalm 19, which begins as a hymn to the glory of creation and moves into a meditation on God's commandments. After expressing how 'the heavens are telling the glory of God, and the firmament proclaims his handiwork', he seems to hesitate and, changing tack, adds, 'There is no speech, nor are there words; their voice is not heard; yet their voice goes out through all the earth.' This is deliberately ambivalent: creation is both vocal and also oddly inarticulate, requiring God's laws and precepts to direct us to him.

In the New Testament, St John proclaims Jesus Christ as the *logos* of God: his creative and self-explanatory word. As such, we might expect Jesus' teaching to resemble notices in the church kitchen and for him to ram home every joke with an emoticon.

Yet the Gospels report that he only ever taught in public using parables. When asked by his disciples why this was so, he quotes the prophet Isaiah, saying 'so that that they may indeed look, but not perceive, and may indeed listen, but not understand'. One can just imagine their faces – *But why would we want that to happen?*

Jesus, we are told, always explained his parables in private to the disciples, but you get the impression this was a wearisome necessity, rather than being the heart of his art. Oscar Wilde wrote of Christ that 'his entire life is the most wonderful poem', because of 'his intense and flamelike imagination', and indeed it seems that, for Jesus, imagination was absolutely central to the perception of truth. To understand a concept as latent as the Kingdom of God, you had to imagine *what it was like*.

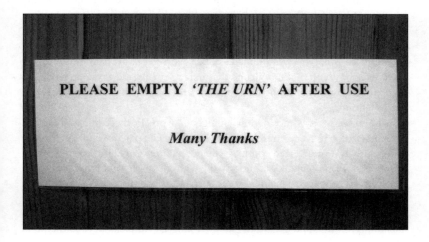

In his essay 'Is theology poetry?' C. S. Lewis affirms that imagination is at the heart of all efforts to make sense, especially language. Christian belief cannot be rephrased without symbolism, because all words are symbols: 'We can make our language duller', he writes, 'we cannot make it less metaphorical.' When Jesus says 'I am the light of the world' or 'I am the true vine', to take two obvious examples, it isn't the literal truth he is telling. However, no Christian would deny that his symbolic description is far truer than had he had said, merely, 'I am extremely significant'. Nobody gives their life for someone who is extremely significant: they might well do so for the light of the world.

Likewise, when Emily Dickinson wrote 'tell all the truth but tell it slant', she was being acute, not obtuse – simply affirming that this is how truth is best perceived. And if the truth *is* slant (which it quite often is), then the arts are needed to do it justice, for they excel at conveying things which aren't straightforward, but are 'more than' we can normally express.

Unless they are being deliberately perverse, artists don't seek to obscure that truth – on the contrary, they tend to be obsessively concerned with getting their subject right. Misrepresentation makes for poor art.

With the creative word of Christ at the centre of its faith, the Church can have confidence in the arts, even if its audience occasionally gets the wrong end of the streamer. But better to risk this than for our pronouncements to be like the preacher I knew, whose sermons were gruelling for those listening because *every phrase* was *emphasized* to *show* how important it *was*. Anyone listening to him felt like a steak being tenderized by an over-zealous butcher. Given the option, I'll have The Fisherfolk.

11. A time of quiet

Dear friends, the season of Lent is upon us. This means that, in services across the land, tea lights are being lit in wild profusion, smooth pebbles are inexplicably passing from pew to pew and the faithful pause to pencil their prayers on Post-it notes. In other words, it is time once again for churches everywhere to try their hand at a spot of *reflective worship*.

To some of you, I suspect, this phrase may provoke the same sense of cold panic as the simple coupling of the words *drama* and *workshop*, but have no fear. Here below, I have furnished you with all you need to conduct your own reflective meditation, which may be read aloud entirely as written, ideally by candlelight.

Naturally it won't work if you read it out like a drill sergeant; you will discover that appropriate tone of voice is everything. The general effect you are trying to achieve is the verbal equivalent of stroking a trout. If that agreeable state is beyond you, imagine yourself instead as a dentist addressing a recumbent three-year-old, and you shouldn't encounter too many problems. I have entitled it, simply, The *filling* station ...

Good evening. At this point in our service, can I simply invite you to pause for a moment as we reflect upon our Lenten journey. This is a time for quiet, a time just to be still and know that *I* am God. No one else talking ... no distractions, just ... the quiet. [*pause*]

Quiet times are so valuable, aren't they? So often in church we long for quiet, but all we hear is a constant stream of meaningless words. We may feel like crying out *if only they'd stop talking* and leave us some space ... But they don't. Here tonight, though, there is space ... no words ... just quiet ...

So often the stresses of the day make us more tense than we realize. And so I just want to begin with a simple breathing exercise. What you need to do is relax and just breathe *in* ... and then *out* [*repeat*]. Maybe you've never done that before. But it can be quite beneficial in all kinds of ways. *Breathing* – in ... and then out.

And tonight I want us to meditate briefly on *emptiness* and *fullness*. What are you full of, I wonder? What am *I* full of? Whatever it is you're full of, can I just encourage you to now become *empty*. Empty heads, empty lives ... that is what we must seek.

The world is so ready to fill our minds with all sorts of things that can't really help – things to do, things to buy – so many worries and cares. But it's a bit like a ... a bath, in a way ... We need to turn off the taps and let the water drain away. So ... if it's helpful you might like simply to turn your taps off with me ... [*make tap turning-off motion with hands*]. Thank you. And then let's just pull the plug out and together make the sound of the water draining away [*you may wish to encourage others here by making the requisite sluurrrpp sound*].

As you take time to become empty, you may find that all manner of *thoughts* and *cares* try to come rushing back in. Simply refuse them and try your hardest – now and in the week ahead – to be though*tless*, care*less* ... And, if you're troubled by sensual thoughts and temptations, then simply resolve to act in a completely senseless way from now on.

To help us in this process I simply invite you now to close your eyes and picture yourself in a *filling station*, a place where people are very much aware of their emptiness, their fullness. In the quiet you might like to say aloud the filling station you have chosen – it might be a garage, it may be a service station [*you may wish to get the ball rolling here by saying, for example, Esso, Leigh Delamere ...*].

As you pull up to the pumps, slowly step out of your car and just take a moment to look at it, to feel it, perhaps to smell it. What is it full of? So many things that need emptying ... perhaps it is your rubbish or your luggage, perhaps it is your ... *oil*. Whatever it is, take a moment in this *filling* station to become empty. Open your doors and bags, undo the sump plug, let it all drain away.

What do you notice about your fellow travellers as you do this, I wonder? Are they also plagued by thoughts and cares? If so, here perhaps is an opportunity to do something truly thoughtless and careless. What they need is a sign that there is another way, just a *symbol* of some sort. What should you do?

Perhaps it might help if you were to *light a candle*. Yes ... perhaps it might. And so, slowly walk round the garage and gently place a lighted candle on each petrol pump. Take a moment to notice how people are responding to your action – what are their expressions, I wonder – are they full of fear, or despair? Maybe it isn't surprising that they are hostile to your carelessness, and, as the sirens sound and you begin another journey, you reflect how hard it is for the world to understand ...

12. Aunty nostalgia

A little while back, I bent my joyful footsteps to Brixton Bus Garage for the farewell of London's famed hop-on, hop-off double-decker bus, the Routemaster. Brixton was the terminus for Route 159, the last to run these mythical beasts, and there gathered an odd congregation of enthusiasts, press and confused passengers, together with those like myself, who seem perversely drawn to such swansongs.

Flasks of coffee were shared, mummified sandwiches unpeeled, and each bus that pulled up would be duly applauded and photographed, the driver beaming in his moment of celebrity. Every so often, a bystander would approach the growling bonnet and pat it fondly, as they might a Golden Retriever. As the route list above the driver's cabin was wound on from 'Marble Arch' to 'Not in Service' there came the unmistakable sound of people quietly deflating.

Each had their own busular memories to relate and I soon realized that, in order to gain access into their twilight circle, I simply had to sidle up and mutter 'sad day' or 'end of an era' to be welcomed as a brother. One such real-time recollection worryingly began in 1939, thus requiring the sort of conversational extraction that is the work of a moment for one schooled in forty years of after-church coffee. As the last Routemaster rattled into the depot and the crowd began to disperse, I paused to overhear one mourner glumly say to his friend, 'Well ... that's it for London now ...'

This doom-laden insecurity about the future is precisely what many people loathe about nostalgic types – that stifling sense that nothing will match up to an imagined and irretrievable past. There is no way forward, only back – except that you can't really go back either. Great.

And yet nostalgia, which we might define as 'history after a few drinks', is increasingly a feature of our age. Literally 'the longing to return home', nostalgia was originally diagnosed as an illness, the word being coined in 1688 by a Swiss doctor who sought a name for the epidemics of homesickness afflicting soldiers fighting abroad. By the late twentieth century, it had mutated into a kind of mass therapy, a comforting refuge from the present, with an entire industry dedicated to feeding our appetite for 'yesteryear'. Instead of curing the nostalgic with leeches or opium, we now treat him to a magazine series that builds up in weekly parts and throws in a free binder.

An intensified nostalgia is the natural offspring of what the geographer David Harvey calls 'space-time compression', his phrase for the giddy pace of change in modern Western society. This, he observes, is 'exciting, stressful and sometimes deeply troubling', as it whisks away the reassuring handrail of all that is certain and familiar.

Admittedly, this has been going on for years – it was no coincidence that the romantic poets started to get all dewy-eyed about hedgerows and rustic follies just as they were being ripped up to build blast furnaces. But in that age, both regress and progress were wedded to a clear spiritual vision of past and future: we were either retreating to Arcadia or advancing to Jerusalem.

But – if you'll allow me – not any more ... The current condition is notable for its lack of a destination, in either direction. With consumer society hurtling forward like a Tesco trolley down a hill, an equally erratic nostalgia is its inevitable counterpart. As Svetlana Boym puts it in her compelling study *The Future of Nostalgia*:

> Modern nostalgia is a mourning for the impossibility of a mythical return, for the loss of an enchanted world with clear borders and values ... a secular expression of a spiritual longing for an absolute, a home that is both physical and spiritual, the edenic unity of time and space before entry into history. The nostalgic is looking for a spiritual addressee. Encountering silence, he looks for memorable signs, desperately misreading them.

If we were again to view outbreaks of nostalgia as a sickness – a kind of cultural senility – we might have genuine cause for alarm at the way in which, like dotty old dears, we have wandered away from home without remembering where we lived.

An informed recovery of our Christian past has to be essential in curing this condition, if only to recall where our society used to reside – and where we once thought we were heading. The whole notion of progress, after all, was a secular eschatology, growing easily from a biblical narrative that saw purpose in history, and portrayed humanity journeying on a clear route from the Garden of Eden to its terminus at the heavenly city.

The uniquely Christian doctrine of the Holy Spirit – also secularized as Hegel's *Zeitgeist* – could be especially useful in jogging our randomly accessed memory. In the New Testament, the Spirit is portrayed as the one who underwrites both past and future by grafting us into Jesus Christ, the clue to history. St Paul calls him the *arrabon* – the down-payment or guarantee of our inheritance.

This is a slippery business to explain, of course, like most things that really matter. Much better to drink it in at a celebration of Holy Communion, where the Church's patent cure is not amnesia, but *anamnesis* – the Greek word used in the Gospels for Jesus' instruction at the Last Supper: 'Do this in remembrance of me.' More than mere recollection, anamnesis is a kind of hopeful commemoration, which looks ahead as confidently as it thinks back. This service is where the longing for home is finally addressed; where – in the threefold acclamation *Christ has died; Christ is risen; Christ will come again* – faith is restored in the passage of time. And where the PA system never works.

In his endearing way, my late father used to call me 'aunty nostalgia', no doubt because of my ability to sigh wistfully before I could talk. In the year I was born there was still – just – steam traction on British railways; there were Lyons Corner Houses and red Morris Minor GPO vans. P. G. Wodehouse was still writing fiction and the Fab Four were still recording. Thereafter, such things became inherently more interesting to me for just having ceased to be – which is precisely the nostalgic's problem. The very lostness, the out-of-reachness of the past, increases your hunger for it.

Nostalgia thus feeds on being insatiable. But it is a tell-tale symptom of a deeper appetite and perhaps the truth is that each of us needs memories with a future, which lamp up the road ahead and lead us home. Memories which, ultimately, can reckon with death. I'm afraid it's that or the bus.

13. Not praying, but sleeping

It was the sort of charismatic prayer meeting where the church looks like a cross between a field hospital and an airport departure lounge. With ministry teams circulating in paramedic clusters, experience has taught me that quick wits and a clear sense of purpose are of the essence. If you don't want to end up stretchered off, you must either steal away home, or – in a less desperate variant of the Stevie Smith poem – assume the guise of one who is not sleeping, but praying.

This time, however, I did want someone to pray with. After several years playing in rock bands next to some fairly bombastic drummers, I had become acutely sensitive to loud and sudden sounds (yes, rock 'n' roll, I gave you the best ears of my life). So, picking a way to the front over my fallen comrades, I approached the man who, from the plastic conference badge on his lapel, had evidently passed the requisite police checks and was in charge of the whole operation. Having carefully explained my problem, whilst he nodded slowly, lips pursed in a compassionate wince, I closed my eyes and settled back to listen for that still, small voice of calm.

'LORD, WE SPEAK *HEALING* INTO THESE EARS,' he bellowed, addressing them directly. Hands cupped to his mouth – and the side of my head – he appeared to be under the impression that I was several miles away.

'… **HEALING,** to these **EARS**,' he added helpfully, at even greater volume, in case I hadn't caught him. Exhibiting a manifestation of the Spirit witnessed neither before nor since, I leapt some ten feet in the air, and became for several weeks thereafter a thing of wonder and praise in devout circles.

Praying with others can be an alarming experience, in whatever church tradition you find yourself. It is a unique form of mediated conversation, where those praying are addressing both each other and God, through the counsels of the Holy Spirit. Like most counselling, this can sometimes have all the awkwardness of an estranged couple who, though sitting next to each other, ask the mediator to tell their partner that, if they want to come home tonight, they have another thing coming.

The most enjoyable of these encounters are evangelical meetings where one person's prayer acts as a kind of doctrinal corrective to that of another. 'Thank you for your abundant grace and love to all people, no matter who they are', one will pray. '*Yes*, Lord ...' another will pray, conceding the point, 'and thank you also that, in your love, you want all people to come to a point of repentance and personal faith.' Such redressing of the balance is only matched for entertainment by prayers in which enthusiasm leads to loss of metaphorical control – the finest example I have witnessed being, 'Lord, we ask that you would literally set us on fire for you.'

Such clangers notwithstanding, praying together informally always makes a positive difference, God being the difference which is always made. A problem shared may be a problem halved, but a problem prayed is a problem released, somehow. Just as most men find it easier to bond or discuss personal matters while addressing something else, like painting a wall, praying together introduces a vital third party who becomes the recipient of things that are otherwise unbearable.

The sense of not being alone is at the heart of all Christian prayers, even those conducted in isolation. It can, of course, be an intensely solitary experience, which no one captured more perfectly than Welsh priest-poet R. S. Thomas, who once likened his prayers to gravel flung against God's bedroom window. 'I would have refrained long since', he observed, with customary detachment, 'but that peering once through my locked fingers I thought that I detected the movement of a curtain.'

Here, as in the Psalms, the person praying may strain for some kind of answer from a God who might seem either absent or deaf, but the very act of hurling problems beyond yourself to the one who invites these missiles becomes transformative. Kneeling is a posture both of worship and despair, making prayer the definitive act of faith.

Crucially it carries us to the one praying in the Garden of Gethsemane, where Christ sweated blood as he asked for the poisoned chalice to pass him by. 'Yet not my will', he prayed to his Father, 'but yours be done.' The prayer of the Christian begins and ends with the prayer of Christ. The Lord's Prayer is nothing less than that – his own prayer life passed on to his followers.

But, like most things relating to him, it is more than a mere stencil – an original for us to trace as best we can. There is always the danger that, in teaching about prayer, the Church treats its members like competitors in *The Generation Game*. In this, you'll recall, television contestants watched an expert do something really well, like set an arm in plaster or ice a wedding cake, and then had to try and do it themselves – usually very badly – whilst the audience and their genial host laughed at them like drains.

Many of us retain a folk memory of the carolling words '*For He is our childhood's pattern ...*' and '*Christian children all must be ... Mild, obedient, good as He ...*' But most Christian children with an ounce of self-awareness will wonder how they can do this. In the New Testament the prayer of Jesus isn't a one-off example, but something which continues as humanity's permanent connection with God. 'He lives for ever to intercede for us', writes the author of the Epistle to the Hebrews, who sees in the risen and ascended Lord a 'great high priest' praying for all those who haven't a prayer on their own.

Not only this, but also he envisages 'a mighty cloud of witnesses' in heaven and on earth, joining in Christ's prayer like revellers at a gig who know every word by heart. Christian prayer is never a solo performance, so there is no need to shout. Rather, we learn to pray at that moment when we dare to launch ourselves off the stage and out onto the sea of hands waiting to hold us up.

14. Down among the dead men

William Walker, ready to descend

Hanging around in cemeteries, as clergy are wont to, has a curious effect upon one's outlook. If they're not careful, those who take funerals for a living can easily end up becoming fun*ereal* – wearing muted colours, and developing a 'doubt they'll make it through the winter' attitude towards any member of their flock who develops so much as a slight sniffle.

It's perhaps not surprising that Hamlet-like ponderings should become second nature when one spends so much time among Yorick and his bedfellows. Here in South London, there are more magnificent Victorian cemeteries than post offices, each one boasting its own roster of notables.

At Beckenham resides Thomas Crapper, the inventor of the water closet, whose joyous name has always seemed to me proof of God's intervention in human affairs. Sadly no chain adorns his headstone. W. G. Grace, the preposterously bearded cricketer, is also pavilioned there, and one William Walker – an early diver whose legacy is to have rescued Winchester Cathedral by diving beneath its waterlogged foundations and gradually shoring them up with concrete.

Every day for nearly six years, and working in total darkness, Walker would plunge to the slimy depths with little more than a rubber air hose to link him to safety. When the cathedral was reopened in 1912 by King George V, the latter proclaimed that Walker had 'saved the cathedral with his own two hands', an accolade Walker dubbed as the proudest moment of his life. After all that, the poor fellow died of influenza – though one imagines burial held few fears for him.

Down the road in West Norwood we find Hiram Maxim, the American entrepreneur who made his fortune by designing the first automatic machine gun. Deaf from exposure to the noise of his weapons, he died in November 1916, just six days after the end of the Battle of the Somme, where over a million and a half soldiers had met their end, many at the muzzle of his invention.

Human stories both charming and terrible abound in these places, building up like the loamy layers of leaves rotting around the tombs. The most alluring are those where fact and myth overlap, like the lady of leisure who, never having shifted from her *chaise longue* during life, insisted on being buried likewise. Within her massive coffin in the catacombs of West Norwood, she reclines on it still, hoping not to be disturbed.

Under this cemetery runs one of the lost tributaries of the Thames, the River Effra, down which Queen Elizabeth is said to have sailed to visit Sir Walter Raleigh at Brixton. Though long entombed beneath the tarmac, the Effra rises again in times of flood and the grass grows verdant along her course. In the mid-nineteenth century, two coffins were discovered floating in the Thames – one of which, upon recovery, was traced back to West Norwood. However, when returned to its resting place, the grave was found to be undisturbed, leading to the only possible conclusion: namely, that the grave had been dug too close to the path of the Effra and the coffin must have subsided into its oily depths. Bumping and gliding underneath the city, it had emerged into the Thames at Vauxhall, where, one presumes, it would have happily bobbed out into the North Sea.

As Lent's long, chocolate-free weeks proceed, we may be reluctant to dwell on Ash Wednesday's morbid refrain, 'remember you are dust and to dust you shall return'. But it is vitally important that the Church can learn to look death steadily in the face, especially in an era so determined to sanitize and ignore it.

Reckoning with the grave gives profundity to our faith, saves it from floating about on the surface. In a solution-based world, it is natural to want to give a positive, solution-based faith, and rush to give answers without letting the deep questions really sink in. But unless we let the end of the human story weigh us, like William Walker, down to the foundations of things, our faith risks a soggy collapse.

Both wit and witness sound shallow when they don't sound the depths – something the Psalms are at pains to explain, as was the ancient writer of the Book of Ecclesiastes. Usually remembered for its 'vanity, vanity, all is vanity' refrain, and – thanks to The Byrds – the phrases from 'Turn, Turn, Turn', Ecclesiastes has another, surprisingly upbeat, chorus illuminating its verses.

Having spent a couple of chapters commenting with heavy irony on how dreadful things are – the biblical equivalent of those 'tell me again how lucky I am to work here' circular emails – the author frequently returns to lines like this: 'Go, eat your food with gladness and drink your wine with a joyful heart, for it is now that God favours what you do.' Amidst his uncomfortable commentary on chaos and death, there is the glowing sense that our stories should be marked by celebration and gratitude: that our mortality need not mean a retreat from life. Underpinning it all is the suggestion of a God who can handle both height and depth. Christian faith can be true to life only because it is first true to death. A life that guffaws forth the news of resurrection is only possible when, like Mary, we have waited long hours by the tomb.

Now, if you'll excuse me, there are some mourners at a certain person's graveside looking a little flushed …

15. All steamed up

Close neighbours in Old Kent Road, London SE1

It was an advertisement using sex to sell kettles that finally convinced me ours was a society in its death throes. The key word bridging this sad synapse was, of course, 'steamy': the thinking presumably being that, driven doolally by desire, satisfaction would only be found by purchasing the sultry spout and curvaceous flex of a Russell Hobbs. In my bachelor days I tried this once, and believe me, it doesn't work.

Within a culture so utterly sold out to the idolatry of desire, so desperate to make everything sexy – including, it would seem, the kitchen sink – the Church faces something like the dilemma of the awkward parent watching a saucy sitcom with her children. They don't want you to laugh along – that would be excruciating – nor do they want you to bluster around with the remote making unintentional puns like 'I think we should have it off now.' So what is there to do, but quietly slip from the room?

An alternative might be to recover the biblical idea that our deepest longings are an echo of our desire for God. This finds its most explicit expression in the post-watershed poetry of the Song of Solomon, included in the canon of scripture as both an affirmation of sexuality and a metaphor of the relationship between God and his people. Not often read aloud in family services, the Song of Solomon is a lidless kettle that doesn't click off, ending on the same note of longing with which it opens – 'come away, my lover'.

While outstanding, it isn't an isolated case of divine and sensual yearnings becoming clouded. 'As the deer pants for streams of water, so my soul pants for you, O God', writes the psalmist, suggesting that human desire originates in a thirst, not for the boiling fleshpots of Egypt – nor even for a nice cuppa – but for eternal refreshment. This is the gist of Jesus' encounter with the Samaritan woman at the well in John's Gospel. Drained and deserted by her sexual history, she hears the shocking suggestion of new fulfilment – the 'spring of living water welling up to eternal life' offered her by Jesus.

St Augustine, the father of Western theology, had a not dissimilar encounter, finding in Christ the resting place for his roving heart. So aware was Augustine of 'the gulf of carnal pleasure' – and so whoopingly had he leapt into it throughout his youth – that his Christian conversion understandably involved a fairly serious renunciation of sensual pleasures. Augustine's dramatic about-turn has affected the way Christians think ever since, and has often meant that, rather than harnessing the wild horses of desire, we have locked them up for fear they'll bolt. Browse through the history of the Western Church for an affirmation of bodily passions and you will be browsing for quite some time: ascetics, yes, of course; puritans – certainly, how many would you like? But lovers? Perhaps you should try next door.

So strong has the fallout been from this perceived legacy of sexual repression that the Church might just need to wait a half-life or two until it says anything further on the subject. Unlikely, you'll admit. Along with Augustine, St Paul is often blamed for this buttoning up of desire so characteristic of the Christian tradition. Yet he seems to have understood these things far better than he is often given credit for. Paul found in Christ a freedom, not from desire as such, but from desires that lead to death – from those drinks which just increase our thirst. Our bodies and our minds, he urged, should be offered to God so that his will, his desire, might begin to refresh and transform our own.

In a similar vein, the founder of the Jesuits, St Ignatius Loyola, offered in his *Spiritual Exercises* various 'rules for the discernment of spirits'. These focus on the believer's need to distinguish between what he called desires of *consolation* and those of *desolation*. The former are those affections which lead to a deepening of our love for others and for God and which bring us true happiness and peace; the latter are those desires which, while initially satisfying, are ultimately destructive of ourselves and our relationships.

Sexual desire does not belong exclusively in either of these categories – quite clearly it can leave us both wonderfully consoled and also deeply desolate. But amidst this moral mire Ignatius is an immensely helpful guide, leading us to nurture those desires which help us 'towards our destination'.

Scripture posits that God is love, but not that Love is god, an assertion that glorifies human love while simultaneously knocking it off its throne. As sex is forever prone to being idolized, the need for chastity – to channel and control our passions – is a song as old as time. And it is best sung, not taught, for dogma rarely does sex justice. Listen to Sam Cooke singing about touching the hem of Jesus' garment and then sweetly soaring into 'You send me' – it's virtually the same song. Marvin Gaye, Al Green, too, howl in a divine ecstasy, summed up in the Reverend's desperate lyric: 'it's you I want, but it's him that I need'.

Regrettably, English Christianity has reared fewer such Soul Men, apart, perhaps, from Jacobean priest and poet John Donne, whose roving fingers penned both sublime sermons and erotic sonnets. The twentieth-century poet, C. H. Sisson, writes in 'A letter to John Donne' of the need to recover the passion in our piety. He disparages the 'evaporated men' who have lately occupied his pulpit and implores Donne to 'Come down and speak to the men of ability on the Sevenoaks platform', and tell them that faith

Is not exclusive in the fools it chooses
That the vain, the ambitious and the highly sexed
Are the natural prey of the incarnate Christ.

Lines worth drinking in, if we can just simmer down.

16. Evandalism

One of the spin-offs of life as a preacher is observing the effect certain words and phrases have upon the faces of one's congregation. Mention some – the word 'coffee', for example – and faces will briefly register the desperate joy of the shipwrecked mariner spying a ship on the horizon after thirty days adrift. Others, like 'theology' will cause something like scales to cover the eyes of the faithful. Still others, like 'perhaps the children would like to use the shakers during this next song' provoke glares of outright mutiny, Mister Christian.

The word 'evangelism' is especially rewarding. To hardened churchgoers, it has a similar effect to that of mentioning a long-outstanding DIY job like re-papering the hallway – making one feel a curious mixture of limpness and guilt. While we recognize the e-word as one of the things that really ought to be done, few of us feel much like doing it and are pretty sure that we'll bodge it up anyway. Can't we just get a little man in to do it for us?

Perhaps we are put off by what can only be called *evandalism* – an indiscriminate dumping of the gospel without thought for the surroundings. When the believer's need to deposit their faith outweighs their love for neighbour, it is rarely good news for anyone. Rather than reveal the Kingdom of God to be a thing of fascination and beauty we push it as though it were a vanload of meat on the turn.

I'm reminded of the scene in a television survival show, where one contestant had just managed to coax a tiny flame from a few dry leaves only for another to bound up and smother it with a great handful of sticks. The first frail flickers of faith need air and careful kindling – some evangelism merely suffocates.

Carpet-bombing the gospel in this way is, above all, a denial of mutual relationship and in stark contrast to the approach Jesus appears to take in the Gospels. No matter how weird, embarrassing or unpleasant people are, there is a sense of them being accommodated by him – even the Pharisees, until they put themselves beyond the pale. It's not toleration so much as an immense *regard*, which gives others the space to come as they are. The remarkable thing, of course, is that he combines this with such a robust and uncompromising message – not an easy balance to achieve.

Doctrinally (another word to watch from the pulpit), this is all about *kenosis*. Kenosis, while sounding like the name of a dubious jazz-fusion band from the 1980s, is instead an invaluable strand of Christian faith. It describes the 'self-emptying' of God witnessed in the incarnation of Christ – his choice to become mortal and to utterly expend himself for others.

This is the feat described in Paul's majestic hymn to Christ in his letter to the Philippians, which explains in lyrical form the detail of what Christians believe about Jesus. 'Your attitude should be the same as that of Christ Jesus', he urges the Church:

> Who, being in the very nature God, did not consider equality with God something to be grasped, but made himself nothing, taking the very nature of a servant, being made in human likeness. And being found in appearance as a man, he humbled himself and became obedient to death – even death on a cross!

Like much about Jesus, it is the complete reverse of how we normally approach life. Each of us is encouraged, with good reason, to make *something* of ourselves, not nothing, and, if we have power, wealth or ability, we use it to *increase*, not decrease. We add to our achievements, we restlessly acquire possessions, we expand – of course we do. As Nelson Mandela rightly observed, 'You are a child of God! Your playing small doesn't serve the world.'

But for Christians, that process of becoming all that we were meant to be can only be perfected in relationships – for the Bible suggests that relationship is at the heart of who we are, and at the heart of who God is. We are made for each other and we are made for God. And in relationships, relentlessly pursuing what I want is a quick recipe for disaster. Every true relationship involves selflessness: actively seeking what is good for the other and learning to deny yourself.

It's fascinating to see how the Bible describes the way in which all things are given life in the very beginning. God's creation in Genesis is not recounted as a huge act of self-indulgence, but rather as if God steps back to allow other things into life beside himself. The very first words of God in scripture are an allowance: 'Let there be light', and so it continues: 'Let the water teem with living creatures ... Let us make man in our own image', and so on. God here appears as a gracious and accommodating host, making room for others (*fish, you come in here, trees – you go wherever you like, spread yourselves around ... Now then, Croydon ... where on earth are we going to put you? Hmmm ...*).

Kenosis is creative; a rare and precious truth which you might like to adopt as a snappy mission statement for your church and dispense with those unnecessary bullet points. When it is overlooked we find evandalism – self-regard, dominance, suffocation.

According to St John's Gospel, disciples of Jesus are sent on their mission in the same way that our Lord was sent into the world by God the Father. We must attempt to 'empty ourselves of all but love', in Wesley's stylish phrase, and preach the good news with the incredible courtesy of Christ. After you, naturally.

17. It's trad, dad

Perhaps the most remarkable thing about working in the Church of England – apart from the strange sense of impending doom that descends at about 6pm each Saturday evening – is the sheer history behind everything one encounters, whether creeds or church hall curtains. I visited a neighbouring church recently and, limbering up in the choir vestry beforehand, noticed a members' address list left casually on a shelf, as if for quick reference. It was dated 1948.

In church, the former things do not pass away, but become gradually more sacred every year; until life becomes so full of former things that there is precious little space for anything else. This is especially true of the sort of former things one would rather do without, as any minister knows who has tried to shift the odd pew or who gently suggests that the dried flowers in the chapel – which have been drying nicely since the early 1990s – might now be removed.

The Church has a peculiar Midas-like gift for transforming everything it touches into tradition, and I always find it a little odd that St Paul doesn't list this alongside all the other gifts in 1 Corinthians: 'Where there are prophecies, they will cease; where there are tongues, they will be stilled; but where there are curious Bible posters of Orang-utans or soft-focus kittens in a basket, they will remain ...'

Do something in church and it immediately has meaning; and if something has meaning, it is extremely hard to get rid of. If you doubt the truth of this, I suggest that, at nightfall, you nip down to your nearest church, where you will espy the vicar scurrying furtively to the tip under cover of darkness, with bulging armfuls of banners, crockery and old Hoovers.

Although the church is exceptionally good (or bad, depending on where you stand) at it, tradition-forming is an inescapable human trait. When the new Kit Kat bar was launched a few years ago, minus its pleasing foil wrapper, Nestle embarked upon a major pastoral offensive to help consumers through this unsettling period. To quote from their press release at the time:

From July, the four finger Kit Kat chocolate bar will be wrapped in a single *funky* plastic foil wrapper like its 'Chunky' counterpart making it even easier to get into Britain's favourite break-time treat. But what about my fun with the foil you may be asking? Fear not, because your Kit Kat rituals are safe. Generations have grown up with the silver foil and paper wrapper of Kit Kat and it has become part of the break-time ritual. However, to make sure that the next generation, who have far less time on their hands, can still enjoy a Kit Kat during their breaks, we have introduced this new convenient packaging. The foil is dead, long live plastic foil!

But for this reassurance, goodness knows what might have happened. Traditions – literally, 'that which is handed down' – are usually invisible, being simply what a culture considers to be normal. Traditions of language and business, traditions of public demonstration or polite behaviour – they are the stitching that hold people together, that enable us to make sense of life as time passes – to know what to do. Traditions will grow whether we like the idea or not. Life would, after all, be almost impossible to live without them: constantly thinking up new ways to do the most ordinary things – never wearing the same shirt twice – never wearing *a shirt* twice. But of course if relentless novelty is one sort of tyranny, then so is the opposite – always doing the same thing. Curiously mixing both ends of the spectrum, American hip-hop producer Damon Dash is renowned for wearing a new pair of trainers every day – his motto, 'Fresh to death', says it all.

Because they are so central to life, changing or ending traditions can be surprisingly stressful, even with something as insignificant as a chocolate biscuit. When major traditions shift – political, scientific or religious – it is like the tectonic plates scraping beneath us. Usually this happens gradually, so that we barely notice life altering until we look back. But not always – and when traditions are suddenly sundered, there are the cultural earthquakes of revolution and reformation.

As Protestants have shown by their endless fragmentation, you don't escape the millstone of tradition by starting afresh. New customs will start to sprout the second time your denomination meets. Perhaps in recognition of this, a useful ready-reckoner emerged among the reformed churches, which has since become a maxim for all matters of religious toleration: 'in essentials, unity; in non-essentials, liberty; in all things, charity'.

The challenge, of course, is to decide which tradition belongs in which category: a question addressed by St Paul in his first letter to the Corinthians. 'For I handed on to you as of first importance what I in turn had received', he tells them: 'that Christ died for our sins in accordance with the scriptures, and that he was buried, and that he was raised on the third day.' Paul uses the same Greek word for 'handed on' earlier in the same letter when underlining the centrality of the Lord's Supper, and we can safely assume these two at least were non-negotiable. On certain other matters splintering their fellowship – notably the eating of food previously sacrificed to idols – he seems less bothered about taking a hard line. 'We are no worse off if we do not eat, and no better off if we do', he writes, with a shrug. One imagines he would have felt similarly about Kit Kats.

Taken in general, the New Testament regards tradition as what it is: a fact of life. It can take us captive, or it can carry us to freedom. Cyprian of Carthage wrote in the third century AD, 'ancient traditions can just be old mistakes': the mark of a mature church, then, is to know what is the essential centre of her faith – and what is merely the wrapper.

18. The beach

In the press of a busy day, we often miss opportunities to pause and allow the deeper meaning of things to become clear. In the sunlight on our landing recently, I was fortunate enough to share one such opportunity with my three-year-old son, who was in a reflective frame of mind. For about a minute no words passed between us as I watched the pasta slowly drying on the carpet and he wrestled with the great thought crystallizing inside. Then, the epiphany complete, he raised his head to me and said, 'Daddy – you're the Lord of the Trees.'

'Yes, son. You are right, I am,' I answered, presently. Taking Our Lord's cue, naturally I then cautioned him not to mention this messianic secret to anyone else. The main thing is that he knows.

In the margins of Lent, perhaps there will be similar moments for you to pause and be granted a glimpse of eternal truth. To help this process along, I have composed another guided meditation that you may like to use – either in private devotion or, better still, in the sort of larger prayer meeting where everyone will treat you with the unquestioning seriousness you deserve.

Good evening. I'm just going to be leading you in a brief guided meditation, to take away the strains of the day: a chance to remember that with faith, *nothing* is possible.

It might help if we begin with some simple breathing exercises. Just become aware of the rise and fall of your breathing and allow the stresses of the day to leave you as you exhale … You may immediately feel the need to breathe in again. Try to resist this temptation and, so that you are completely relaxed, simply continue to breathe out while I count: one … two … three … four … five … six … seven [*continue counting for as long as you feel is necessary for people to be resting in peace*].

And now, remaining calm, I want you to shut your eyes and imagine that you're on a beach: a lovely sandy seaside, somewhere in Britain. In the quiet, perhaps you'd like to name which seaside it is – either out loud or in the silence of your hearts [*feel free to mention one or two locations to encourage others – Frinton … Cleethorpes … etc.*].

What's the weather like on the beach? Is it raining? Yes, of course it is. What do you notice as you wander along the beach? Looking up you see a flock of lovely seagulls swooping and diving overhead. It's almost as if they have been put there just for you, as a delightful gift.

One of them appears to have a gift for you, too. Something inside you wants to raise your hand to your forehead to wipe it off, but how wrong that would be. No, you will leave it there, you will accept the gift – and perhaps say aloud, with me – *thank you, my seagull friends* [*repeating, with emphasis*], *thank you, my seagull friends*.

In a sense, you are now one of them, and so you begin to gently jog along the beach and, together with your new friends, start to flap your arms up and down … Perhaps you'd all like to do this now – just flap your arms up and down like … like a nutter. No one will mind – all our eyes are closed …

Now then, here's a lovely scene. In front of you is a family group building a wonderful sandcastle. What time and care they have taken with it – all those shells gently pressed into the walls, the seaweed and driftwood carefully collected and pushed into place. A little flag flutters from the tower – and the father and his children step back to admire their work. But something is wrong, somehow, and you feel sad … Then you notice what it is: their sandcastle has *walls* around it … walls to keep others out. All that beauty and creativity – shut in behind high walls. What a shame …

In an instant, you realize that you cannot leave this scene. These people need your help – to take their walls down, to be freed from their defensive ways. So, with the seagulls' lovely gift freshly dripping from your forehead, arms still flapping up and down, you gently swoop across … and *flatten* the walls of the sandcastle, liberating the seaweed and driftwood from its sandy prison and strewing them around the beach to share with everyone.

A strange feeling of peace comes over you having done this – but not, you notice, over the father and his children whom you have helped. What do you notice about them? Are some of them crying? Are some of them cross? How hard it is for others to break down their walls – how hard it is for them to thank you for having helped them.

But a seed has been sown in their lives, nevertheless, something they won't forget. And as they pick you up and hurl you bodily into the sea, you realize the need to flap your arms again – this time in a different way …

19. I'm loathin' it

Without disclosing my reasons, I recently had the privilege of becoming a member of the Austin Maestro and Montego Owner's Club, an association devoted to a pair of peculiarly rust-prone and hard-to-love sons of the late British motor industry. As soon as the club magazine *Monstro* (oh yes) plopped onto my doormat I realized with a shiver that, for the first time, I belonged to something less cool than the Church of England. An experience like that puts things into perspective, I can tell you.

A discerning glance at photos of the organizing committee showed me two things: (a) that none of the membership (of which I was number 243) were likely to have been among the first to be picked for school sports teams, and (b) that each cared not a jot for their cars' woeful reputation. This breezy disregard for how the world at large might perceive their cause was encouraging, even if parts of the car did keep snapping off in my hand.

For one of the more aggravating features of our age is an absurd degree of self-consciousness on the part of organizations and institutions. The most obvious, and irritating, indicator of this trend is the strapline – that phrase or sentence designed to stir up the corporate spirit. Straplines have been around for years, of course, but with the unstoppable reach of branding into every area of life, they have sprouted everywhere. Even no-nonsense bodies like the British Army, whose beefy strapline is *Be the best* (at fighting, presumably), have to parade the blighted things, along with sensible agencies like the National Trust, which now clasps us to its powdery bosom with the gushing *For ever, for everyone*.

Some straplines are archly hip, as with McDonald's' *I'm lovin' it*, whereas others are plain mystifying – enter the catastrophic *Doing the right thing* from British Gas, mercifully abandoned after a couple of years confounding a public who simply wanted their meter read, not to be offered moral guidance.

The purpose of all this drivel is, as we know, to lend organizations a more accessible, personal face and to enhance the consumer's sense of belonging, in order for business to boom. A kind of covenant is being sought, along the lines of 'you will be our sort of person and we will be your sort of people'. The general effect, however, is of being roundly patronized or jollied along.

It's also just a bit embarrassing when respectable businesses turn all coy and need to talk about *us*. My heart sinks when I realize that another organization which previously required just a quarterly cheque now also wants me to *like* them. Washing my hands in a hospital toilet the other day, even the hand towels were making advances, with Johnson Diversey pledging that *Clean is just the beginning*. I decided not to risk it and fled with dripping hands, half expecting a wad of paper towels to be turning down the covers for me when I arrived home.

I shan't go on. But the interesting – and unnerving – thing for the Christian is that the New Testament is crammed with corporate-speak of one sort or another. You only have to ruffle its Rizla-esque leaves to find you are defined by your relation to the whole – as a member of God's household, a living stone in a spiritual temple, a body part in the corpus of Christ. St Paul, especially, pushes the metaphors to their creaking limits to show that, together, we are 'in Christ'.

But, in the antithesis of consumerism, this extreme degree of belonging is achieved, not by having your every need met, nor by enhancement of your lifestyle, but by gaining the glorious knack of putting yourself second. Only by obeying the command to put God and neighbour first is the Church enabled to be a body made of different members, defined only by its centre, Christ, and not by the type of people who may belong to him – or, indeed, who would normally want to belong to each other. In other words, unless your church car park is a healthy mix of Leyland and Lexus, something may be wrong.

This is just the sort of generous catholicity straplines tend to qualify and, thereby, restrict, for they raise a perimeter fence that requires the outsider first to ask 'am I that sort of person?' before gaining access. The same could be said for the particular agony and hilarity of local church advertising, which can become a kind of day-glo barbed wire around places of worship that the passer-by might otherwise drop into.

The Church can never be completely comfortable with marketing itself, for that requires the type of corporate self-consciousness we are rightly uneasy with. The original promoter of Jesus was, after all, John the Baptist, whose slogan was 'I must decrease so that he may increase'.

I live, however, in daily fear that my own Anglican church, alarmed by a Montego-like tendency to disintegrate, may, even as I write, be devising its own strapline in a misguided bid to boost membership. You might like to mull over this nightmare prospect and consider the rotten fruit such an exercise would assuredly bear. I've had a few ideas – *Love will tear us apart*, possibly, or, for our more conservative brethren, *I'm leavin' it*, but the only one I'm currently happy with is, The Church of England: *it's not about us*.

20. That's the way to do it

In order to be remembered by history as A Thinker, it has long been evident that what you really need is not a huge library of books to your name but a pithy maxim or theorem, which neatly captures a bit of the truth and lodges it in the popular memory by reference to some commonplace everyday thing – a greenhouse, say, or a teapot.

So we have Occam's Razor, Schrödinger's Cat, Maxwell's Demon (commonplace or not, depending on your theology) and my personal favourite, Morton's Fork. John Morton was a fifteenth-century Archbishop of Canterbury, who, when doubling as Lord Chancellor, was tasked with outlining Henry VII's crushing tax burden on the populace. No one, rich or poor, could be exempt from this, he said (no doubt with pastorally sensitive body language), because – and here come the prongs – those who lived in luxury were obviously able to pay up, whilst those who lived frugally must have ample savings put by and so could equally afford to give generously to the king. Either way you're skewered – that's Morton's Fork. Nice to recall a time when the Church of England could really speak with relevance on money issues, you'll agree.

But none of these forks, cats and razors can compete in terms of impact with Plato's Cave, the great illustration he used to explain his theory of Ideas or 'forms'. In this he likened people to prisoners forever chained up in a dark cave who gaze at the shadows on the wall cast by a fire burning behind them. Somewhat improbably, I feel, there is a kind of puppet show being staged in front of the fire behind them, but, because of their chains, all they can view is the shadow play of Mr Punch hilariously tugging sausages out of the crocodile's belly.

The prisoners, Plato explains, are, quite literally, bound to mistake the shadowy appearance for reality because, without turning their heads, they would know nothing of the actual 'form' behind it. So it is in our world, he suggests: the eternal truth of things is invisible to us while we are incarcerated in space and time. All that we can sense are fleeting shadows of the real thing.

I wonder. What strikes me as ironic and slightly mind-bending about this is that Plato relies on ordinary things (caves, puppets etc.) to reveal the truth that ordinary things can't reveal the truth. Which just goes to show that big ideas only work if they can also be small ideas – even if your big idea is that small ideas aren't much use. Truth must be tethered down to earth – not just to help explain it, but to be true in any sense. 'No ideas but in things', as I would have said, had not William Carlos Williams got in first.

The relationship between the particular and the universal is one of the great themes in Western thought, and it seems fairly obvious that universal effects rely on particular causes, whether the apple bouncing off Newton's hat or the split atom that flattened Hiroshima. To reverse the old hippie dictum, it's surely right to Think Locally, Act Globally – for, in this world at least – the local is the mother of the universal.

If the truth lies on our doorstep, then the particular details of life and our responses to them are of the greatest significance. Stepping out of my house, I might turn left up to heaven or right into hell (and Penge, as it happens).

Anyone who holds fast to this theorem – which history must know as Rumsey's Porch – should prick up their ears when St Paul points to Jesus Christ as the agent of God's cosmic plan 'to bring all things in heaven and on earth together'. The belief that this one man, from a single time, place and culture, could be said to save the world has often been objected to as the Scandal of Particularity. But far from discounting him, I've always felt that the particularity of Jesus – his very *localness* – made him eminently qualified to be saviour of the world.

Set aside the plain fact that, whatever one might think of him, this lone Galilean clearly *has* had universal impact on an unrivalled scale. The point is that, in a world where Crick and Watson can discover the secret of DNA in a Cambridge cycle shed, one might equally expect to stumble upon the secret of eternal life in a Bethlehem barn.

We sometimes assume that, if God existed and desired to make himself known, then he would do so in an unmistakably huge way, as if that was how things worked round here. But it palpably isn't. Life is chaotic and contingent: it's viral and timely, and if God created it that way, is it so shocking that his self-revelation should follow the same pattern? One might even say he would have to act locally if his truth was to be in any sense real; but that would mean making God subject to my theorem and, on balance, that would be unwise, especially as a clergyman.

But in his dealings with this world, God is particular before he is universal; his kingdom consistently likened by Jesus to a tiny thing that grows large or has significance far beyond its size: a mustard seed flourishing into the largest of shrubs; a priceless pearl that you would sell your grandma for.

Christ is the significant detail of history, and those who seek him must start by thinking small. In the Book of Leviticus, the massive, mysterious idea of holiness – being like Almighty God, no less – is achieved by the simple manner in which you plough a field. Leave some unturned ground by the edges, it says, so that the landless poor can glean some of your harvest. Do this and you will live.

If you'd rather not, I gather Archbishop Morton has some alternatives ...

21. When a knight won his spurs

To understand the romantic conundrum of the St George's flag, listen again to cross-legged assembly favourite *When a Knight Won his Spurs*. Stirring the children of Albion to life's high adventure, it carries the misty reminder that 'back into storyland giants have fled, and the knights are no more and the dragons are dead'. Because old opponents are thus slain and shrouded in myth, England's emblem is handily free for conscription into any fresh campaign the nation considers appropriate. The obvious question for those who seek to run the red rag up the flagpole is, which one?

St George has always been a sword for hire and, apart from England, is the patron saint for a dozen other countries, including – slightly awkwardly – Germany. He is also the saint with portfolio for soldiers, archers and saddlers and, apparently, helps those suffering from leprosy, plague and syphilis. Clearly, he got around.

St George's flag has likewise long been traded, with possible origins in that of Genoa, adopted by the City of London in the twelfth century to claim Genoese protection for their ships in the Mediterranean. At much the same time, the design was taken up by English knights fighting in the crusades, who claimed it as their own, provoking a typically English spat with the French, who thought it should be theirs. Despite the pope stepping in as referee, it took a great deal of shirt-swapping before the England away kit was finally established.

Back home, St George's cross did not emerge victorious until the Reformation of the sixteenth century, when all other saints' banners were abolished. Since that time, as both national flag and ensign of the Church of England, it has fluttered from steeples as a restless crest for the bond between church and state.

Various threads have woven to make the cross of St George fly high again in recent years. The rise of regional nationalism in Scotland and Wales and the circling debate about multiculturalism – with its correspondent fears about 'Englishness' – are significant here. But it is as a sporting icon that the flag has become so prominent, with a staggering 27 per cent of the adult population having bought one during the 2006 FIFA World Cup. Riding on the shoulders of this exuberance, the red cross now fronts a substantial campaign to introduce April 23rd, St George's Day, as a national holiday in England, its website clamouring for 'our day' to be recognized.

The question abides, however, who 'we' are – which is precisely what flags are designed to identify. The challenge for St George's Day campaigners, alongside a lingering shadow the flag casts to the far-right, is how to include everyone in a symbol which is all about taking sides. In the clear-cut divisions of war or football the flag works perfectly: less so in the polite fight to establish who or what constitutes the English people today.

But then crosses always aim at the union of opposing forces and St George himself is really more 'them' than 'us' – a Turk, of all people, who fought as a soldier in the Roman Empire and became a Christian martyr after refusing to sacrifice to pagan gods. The story about the dragon didn't appear for another thousand years, but stuck fast in the heart of a nation that loves to tackle imaginary monsters.

What unites people under a flag, after all – apart from shared time and territory – is a common vision, without which, the Book of Proverbs reminds us, the people perish. The vision of England, blurry and bloodshot, is struggling to focus on a new noble cause. A clue to finding one remains in the strains of the old school hymn, with its rallying cry to:

Let faith be my shield and let joy be my steed
'Gainst the dragons of anger, the ogres of greed;
And let me set free with the sword of my youth,
From the castle of darkness, the power of the truth.

These sentiments, though high-blown and hard to reach as a flag on a spire, could be somewhere to start.

22. The pigeon of peace

When fully parked, the stretch of road outside my window is one-and-a-half cars wide, and in it I can see a pair of motorists, horns locked in rage, refusing to engage reverse. This kind of face-off happens several times a day and occasionally boils over into real violence. Short of strapping on an acoustic guitar and gently singing to them, it's not easy to know how to respond.

Many disputes, local and global, are sparked by a perceived lack of space, victory often going to those who, like the airline passenger next to you happily taking up both armrests, have the impertinence or bulk required to spread themselves around.

For the greater part of its history, theological controversies within the Church have also focused on spatial questions – principally that of how and whether the creator God 'made room' for himself within the space and time occupied by Jesus Christ. Metaphysical arguments, like physical ones, have to be fought with the weapons available at the time. So, instead of reaching in the back of the van for a baseball bat, the Fathers of the early church got to grips with Aristotle.

In Aristotle's scheme of things, the space for something or someone was always defined by its boundary – nothing could be real without being limited or contained in some way – even the universe itself. But how could an infinite God be contained within one particular man? This question nearly tore apart the early church and continued to flare up through medieval times into the Reformation period, when it focused on the issue of God's presence in the bread and wine consecrated at communion.

For most modern passers-by, such feuds are even harder to fathom than the causes of the Great War. We view their huge historical turbulence with disbelief, wondering what on earth the fuss was about. A typically religious feud about nothing real.

But in part, at least, they were grappling with one of the most substantive questions of any age: namely, how can our convictions capture the truth without imprisoning it? All words and concepts are nets for catching truth – all versions of the ancient Sunday school joke where the inquisitive child asks his teacher whether God is everywhere. When she agrees that yes, he is, instead of leaving it at that, the little squirt keeps pursuing the matter until he is clear that God is also on the desk in front of him, at which point he cups his hands and, making a quick grab, proudly declares 'Got him!'

From the standpoint of Christian belief, the child was both right and wrong. Yes, God was close as his pencil case, but no, he hadn't trapped him like a butterfly in a net. The more of the truth he grasped, the more he would find it still fluttering ahead of him. Jesus promised that, after his death, believers would be 'led into all truth', not given it for display, pinned like a specimen to a board.

Along with the Sunday school teacher, we need ways of confidently telling the truth which leave 'man with his mind ajar', as the poet Denise Levertov memorably put it. Sceptical of any transcendent reality, much twentieth-century thought denied that language could do this – arguing, like Lewis Carroll's Humpty Dumpty, that 'when I use a word, it means just what I choose it to mean – neither more, nor less'.

But what if our words mean more than we can say? The great councils of the early church chose theirs with extreme care, for the creeds they framed were a kind of doctrinal peace-treaty. By rejecting a 'containerized' version of space and time, the Nicene Creed affirmed that there was, in effect, 'room' in Jesus Christ both for humanity and divinity, and that God could be fully present in Christ without negating or limiting his presence elsewhere. In other words, ultimate truth was not sealed off from – or indeed into – this world – but was both with us and beyond us. The truth is plain to see, but, like the risen Christ, we'll never lock it in.

King Solomon touched upon a similar theme when he dedicated the first temple in Jerusalem about three thousand years ago. Pondering the irony of making an earthly 'house' for a boundless God, he prayed, 'But will God indeed dwell on the earth? Even heaven and the highest heaven cannot contain you, much less this house that I have built.' His wisdom lay in acknowledging the limitations of a human structure while remaining confident of real encounter with the divine.

Modern Britain has its own doctrinal battles to fight over which kinds of truth can be accommodated within her boundaries. Liberal society, temperamentally averse to conflict, has generally sought to tolerate diverging worldviews. But the one who smothers with harmony from fear of discord is rarely any good in a contest, ending up less like the dove of peace than one of those idiot pigeons that blunder onto the centre court at Wimbledon on finals day.

Solomon's wisdom was famously defined by his mediation in a dispute where the opponents couldn't both be right. Two prostitutes were brought into him, each claiming to be the mother of a single baby and insisting that the other had stolen it from them. So Solomon called for a sword and commanded that the child be divided in two, with half being given to each woman. One woman pleaded with the king for the child's life – urging that it be given up to her opponent rather than be slain. The other, we read, consented to the king's dreadful suggestion, saying, grimly, 'It shall be neither mine nor yours; divide it.' Solomon had heard enough – 'Give the first woman the living boy', he commanded, 'she is his mother.'

Some disputes, like certain stretches of road, are simply not wide enough to contain parties travelling in opposite directions. Unless you can transcend the boundaries, there are only two real options: confidently advancing within limited space or releasing the clutch on what may rightfully be yours and reversing. But, as history shows, neither may avoid a scrap.

23. The waiting room

For the majority of the population, entering a church is a similar kind of experience to that had by the majority of churchgoers upon entering a gym. There are the same unfamiliar smells and equipment; the same uncertainty about what to do and when; the same intense desire not to look an idiot. Despite being welcomed within an inch of their lives, newcomers can't avoid this vulnerability, and all one can really do is make the transition as natural as possible.

I once heard of a church where anyone unlucky enough to be attending worship for the first time was invited to stand up during the service while the cordial cleric fixed them with a rictus smile and the congregation sang each guest a welcoming chorus. This kind of special treatment is, I suppose, kill or cure – you'll either leave feeling like a red-carpet VIP or like setting up a standing order to the National Secular Society.

The understandable temptation for churches is to try and reduce the difference between church and everything else people do: they'll show World Cup football on a big screen, for example, or serve real ale in the crypt. While sound good sense as part of its social calendar, this is more problematic when applied to worship.

Worship, whilst always starting from where we are, should take us up from the mundane into something qualitatively different. In other words, it should enable transcendence: the experience whereby we are lifted out of our normal situation in order to see it in another light, and return to it renewed.

As on an airline flight, the most insecure parts of the transcendent experience are taking off and landing. These times require special care and attention in order to integrate worshippers with the real world, and enable them to sniff the air outside again when the service is over.

Anyhow, in order to assist your congregation in this adjustment back into normality, here is another guided meditation. You know the drill – simply lower the lights, adopt the manner and vocal tone of a lobotomized nanny and let the silence do the rest. I have entitled this one The Waiting Room.

Good evening. Welcome to our next guided meditation for Lent. As I lead you on this spiritual journey, it might be helpful just to relax completely each part of your body in turn … Starting with your head … your ears … your teeth … your *hair* … just let it relax … Is any part of your body still tense? Any of your muscles? Muscles are useful, yes, but not tonight … And if relaxing them means that you start to … to *dribble* … or *slump* over onto the floor, then just let that happen … your neighbour won't mind … and if they do, just gently but firmly … *kick them.*

Here in this place, gathered together, we are like *one body* – and so just become aware of those next to you in all their wondrous complexity: imagine all their bodily functions busying themselves only inches away from you … and realize that, in a very real way, you are part of their body. In a way also this ceiling and these walls are like a huge great covering of *wonderful skin* and we are here inside as … *body parts.*

In the quiet, beneath this great skin, it may be helpful to say out loud which body part you are … [*at this point you might like to encourage other folk to contribute by naming aloud various body parts – pelvis … epiglottis … and so on*].

And now, remembering that you are a body part, I want you to imagine that you are now leaving the safety of the church and entering … a doctor's surgery.

At the surgery, you are at the head of a long queue and the receptionist is asking your name … How superficial your old name seems to you now, how isolated from the rest of the body. And so you simply pause for a moment and tell her your *new* name, your *body* name.

She appears not to have heard and asks you your name again. How slow people in the world are to understand, how dull they are. How easy it would be to give her the answer she *wants* to hear, and how keen the people waiting behind you seem to be that you do so. But that is not your way and, with a helpful smile, you simply repeat your *real* name – I am *legs* … I am *kidney* … [*pause*].

Touchingly, the man behind you in the queue also appears to have a new name for you … It too is a body part. You smile and thank him, glad that, all around you, people are beginning to understand …

With this seed so profoundly sown, you leave the lively hubbub behind you and proceed into the doctor's consulting room. For all his knowledge he looks a worried man. For all the books on his shelf he doesn't appear to realize that you are part of *his* body. *How can you help him, do you think?* Surely, mere speech won't be enough … No, you will need to *make contact* in a more real way. And so, without a word, simply approach him and begin to feel the contours of his face with both your hands … his ears … his *nose* …

How is he responding? What do you notice about his complexion or the tone of his voice? Rather wonderfully he appears keen to make contact with you now, too, and slowly you become aware that you are being carried out into the street by a whole host of bodies, all functioning as one. So once again, just allow your muscles to relax completely, and let them take you where they will. Your work here is done ...

24. Mighty rivers
of praise

Dance, then, wherever you may be,
I am the Lord of the dance, said he.

This tune has a lot to answer for. Time's dubbing may have rendered the hymn harmless and even faintly endearing, but those batty lyrics and jaunty beat were as the hips of Elvis in their impact upon the postwar church, heralding a departure from Proper Hymns towards Something a Little Livelier.

As a small child, I would watch enthralled as our organist – vanquished in a battle of wills with the vicar – would dispense with 'Lord of the dance' by charging through it as if his cassock were aflame. The Lord – who had hitherto been rehearsing a gentle foxtrot – became whisked into a frenzied tango, which reached its climax as the organist hurtled to the last chord and proceeded to fling the hymnbook over the back of the organ in disgust, whereupon it landed with a clatter.

The poor incumbent would have had an easier time had he attempted to introduce *Lady Chatterley's Lover* onto the church bookstall. He might read out his shopping lists for sermons and the faithful would nod appreciatively and comment with enthusiasm on his choice of text. But strike a jarring note musically and each would look as though they'd swallowed a wasp.

Forty years and a thousand choruses later, an uneasy truce exists between traditional and popular styles in many churches, brokered in part by a new generation of British hymnbooks gamely striving to integrate the best of both. Nevertheless, most lean towards either Classic FM or Radio 2 in their repertoire, which would be fine if church services were solely there for our listening pleasure.

But what we sing affects more than our mood. Crucially, it also shapes our belief – a truth which hymn writers like Wesley and Watts harnessed so successfully that we are still, as it were, singing their praises. Lyrics seep down into us and stay there whether we like it or not: it is to my great anxiety that I could, for example, recite from memory the words to *Total Eclipse of the Heart* far more readily than I could most of the Psalms.

The principle at work here is that of *lex orandi lex credendi* (either of which, it occurs to me, could pass for names of American renewal songwriters) – 'the law of praying is the law of believing'. Viewed historically, our hymnody is a fascinating index of that belief in any given period. Rummage amongst Victorian hymnals and you might find something like this:

Jesus is the captain of the seas,
A titan o'er the foam:
Who fires his broadside sure and true
And makes Guildford his home.

Jesus is the guardian of the isles,
A fellow just like us:
Who plays a straight bat o'er life's pitch
And won't stand any fuss.

Jesus is the champion of the strong,
Who tends e'en lame and needy:
Who helps the poor, but not too much,
In case they just get greedy.

Speed ahead to the present day, though, and the menu is rather different. Let me share with you one of my own recent compositions entitled 'Make me an instrument of your face':

Make me an instrument of your face,
Jesus, melt these tears of stone.
Touch, O touch my life, O Lord,
Until I'm drenched in praise –
And hold me
(Women): Hold me
(Men): Hold me
(Women): Hold me
(Men & women together): Hold me to your throne.

Let me really feel your heart,
And not just in a metaphorical sense.
I want to see it, shining forth,
So that the world may know

You've freed me
(Women) Freed me, [*etc., as above*]
(All) Freed me from intelligence.

And let a mighty river flow,
Like rushing flames throughout this nation, Lord.
We can't quite envisage what that would look like –
Nor, indeed, are we clear why it ought to happen – but wash me
(Women) wash me
(Men) wash me
(Clergy) wash me
(Single mothers) wash me
(Drunks at the back) WASH ME
(All) Wash me till I'm whole.

© HeartShine Music 2009

Gung-ho imperialism and laboured intimacy are two themes which clearly show how hymns reflect cultural as much as doctrinal norms. This is bound to be the case, but to save church music from being reduced to personal taste or spiritual faddery, we have to begin by considering God, not ourselves. The first question is not *what should we sing?* It is *who are we worshipping?*

If Christians hold God to be both utterly beyond us yet also closer than our breath, our music must reflect that breadth and not make him a mere overhead projection of our desires.

A tall order, admittedly, but perhaps the only real antidote to hymnbook-flinging is to take the advice of that grandmother of all choruses and 'turn your eyes upon Jesus'. For most of us do indeed appear strangely dim in the light of his glory and grace. Let's sing that one twice.

25. The Jesus nut

'It must be nice to believe that there's a spiritual side to life,' ventured the pleasant woman next to me at the party, between mouthfuls of goat's cheese. Whilst neatly tossed into the conversational void that often opens up after vicars reveal their day job, her words hung in the air like balloons half-filled with helium. And I genuinely couldn't think how to respond. So instead of telling the truth – which is, that I don't think that there is a spiritual side to life – I just said, weakly, 'Yes, I suppose it is' and stared down at my mixed leaves.

More often than not, religious faith is considered as a kind of appendix to normal life – an application, a plug-in, enabling you to do extra things. Churches don't exactly discourage this attitude, it's fair to say. The vast majority of our advertising promotes Christianity on the basis of what it can add: wayside posters of jigsaws saying 'Missing peace?' through to giant hoardings asking if there isn't more to life than this. Christ becomes another thing that we haven't got, but must get, because he can add peace or forgiveness, or a 'spiritual dimension' to our lives.

This is not only misleading to those outside the Church but dreadfully sapping for those in the pew, whose faith must always be about striving for 'more than' the life they've been given, whose mystery and promise is staring them in the face. Many believers feel that, because their spiritual life is ordinary, they must only have the basic handset and really ought to upgrade.

Paul's letter to the Colossians was written to a church under just such pressure. The heresy known as Gnosticism (as in gnome, not gnu) was beginning to appear, which offered a 'higher' level of religious knowledge than most entry-level Christians were able to achieve. Under the influence of Greek thought, Gnostics viewed humanity as trapped in the material world – a unfortunate state which could only be transcended by access to certain kinds of esoteric knowledge, or 'gnosis'. Without it, you really didn't have a clue.

Paul attacked this in his letter by portraying Christ, not as a means of escape from the world, but as the one who makes sense of it. In a remarkable passage, he describes him as, effectively, the agent of creation – 'He is before all things and in him all things hold together.' All things – couscous, crocodiles, the double helix, the A13, Saturn, the South Pole, Noel Edmonds, Constable, Dunstable, everything. Including, it would seem, helicopters.

Most helicopters are kept aloft by a single nut or pin which holds the main rotor blade to the mast. Without this component, the whole mechanism falls apart, and it happens to be called The Jesus Nut. Some think the term was first used by US troops in Vietnam; others attribute it to Igor Sikorsky, religious author and pioneer of the first modern helicopter. Sikorsky was a devout Russian Orthodox Christian, but I doubt that he had a spiritual side to his life. Instead, he had a Jesus nut that held everything together.

Jesus Nut from a Bell helicopter

As far as Christianity is concerned, there is no 'religious sphere', nothing supernatural that isn't also natural. As Dietrich Bonhoeffer writes, 'sharing in Christ we stand at once in both the reality of God and the reality of the world. The reality of Christ comprises the reality of the world within itself.'

Like a window, or a lens, faith isn't something you should look at so much as look through. Whenever you look at it, it just seems smudged and rather odd, because religion is a means of viewing the world, not an end in itself, thank goodness. Indeed, there is a strong case for saying that the closer you get to Jesus Christ, the more invisible your religion should become.

This is a refreshing theme in religious art and literature of the Reformation period, when the scriptures were released from being the possession of a spiritual elite, so that men and women could learn for themselves how they might 'do everything for the glory of God', as St Paul exhorted the Corinthians.

William Tyndale, the man who first translated the Bible into English, wrote that 'if our desire is to please God, pouring water, washing dishes, cobbling shoes and preaching the word is all one'. There was no divide between the sacred and the secular – heaven could be found, as George Herbert famously wrote, in the 'ordinarie'. Or, as he expressed it in his hymn-poem 'Teach me, my God and King:

Teach me, my God and King,
in all things thee to see,
and what I do in anything
to do it as for thee.

A man that looks on glass,
on it may stay his eye;
or if he pleaseth, through it pass,
and then the heaven espy.

To promote Jesus as an additional course to the main meal of life marginalizes him and makes faith purely a matter of consumer taste: for the nuts who like that kind of thing. It also blinds us to the spirituality of the commonplace and effectively prevents it from being redeemed. Eternal life is not a complimentary mint after the banquet is over; it is the totality of existence lived in the light of Christ, now and hereafter. The hope of pie in the sky is an excellent one, and any fool would want a slice. But we are unlikely to experience any such thing if, in our folly, we have neglected first to see the sky in the pie.

26. Unoriginal sin

Musing for Lent on the meaningless and unending pain of existence, one's thoughts naturally return to schooldays, and especially the perverse talent we boys displayed for inflicting Neronian torments upon one another.

Whether this was acquired behaviour or simply the inherited wisdom of former generations is hard to judge; but certainly the names of these infernal practices – the Chinese burn; the dead leg; the nipple screw – imply a murky provenance somewhere around the reign of King Arthur.

Often this torture took the form of a dull game called 'pass it on'. The stratagem – not the product of a fertile imagination – was essentially utilitarian: one child would choose a treatment from the aforementioned suite of options and inflict it upon his neighbour, accompanied by the gloomy refrain 'pass it on'.

By turning his attack into a game, the assailant thus excused himself from any retribution and ensured that his injury of choice would spread from desk to desk like a flu virus. The general effect was that of a moderately painful and extremely irritating Mexican Wave. Anybody could have stopped it and either not passed it on or passed it back (with interest), but of course no one ever did. We all just passed it on.

The wearying, cyclical nature of such things holds true in myriad ways beyond the school gates, from copycat consumerism and gang loyalty to the various forms of abuse and addiction that domino down the generations. Sin is, and ever has been, contagious, habit-forming and utterly predictable.

The least harmful and most amusing confirmation of this in recent times is without doubt the ill-fated Cambridge Green Bike Scheme of the early 1990s. Devised by the bearded idealist then leading the city council, the scheme arranged for bicycles from the police pound to be painted green and set in racks around the city. The idea was that anyone needing to travel could simply pick up a green bike and cycle it to the rack nearest their destination where they would, in a spirit of neighbourliness, leave it for the next person to use, possibly inflating the tyres for them before they strolled off. With glorious inevitability, by the end of the first day, all 300 bicycles had been stolen. Most residents never even saw one.

In one stroke, the heroic failure of the Green Bike Scheme demonstrated both the Fall of Man and the flaw in all utopian visions. But it was the very 'I could have told you this would happen' nature of its downfall which affirmed how, at heart, sin is profoundly *un*original, thriving by implication and association, on each of us being and doing exactly the same as everyone else has been and done before.

Abandoned shopfront in Thornton Heath, Croydon

It is the virtuous who are the true originals: those who add realism to the idealism of the Green Bike guru and count the cost of their nonconformity. Like Rosa Parks, for example, the ordinary church member who, 'tired of giving in', refused to budge on the Montgomery omnibus, and so ignited an entire civil rights movement.

Such people seem not to have heard the instructions. Quite often, they also end up getting killed, which is deeply unsettling for a Body of Christ sitting rather too comfortably. Their example, like the passion narrative it emulates, asks us what we would do in similar circumstances. It sets us among the soldiers dicing and baiting beneath the cross and asks whether or not we will play along.

In order to square up to sin's sad circus, the Christian Church opted early on to make the calendar itself contest the way we live. This opened up the year like a board game, which led the faithful on a seasonal tour through the life and death of Christ, who took what was tortuous and declined to pass it on.

Lent, whose drab colours and self-denial might at first glance appear to be the Old Kent Road of the Church's Monopoly set, in practice proves to be its Mayfair. It comes, however, with a price tag to match.

27. A few short questions

Working for a spell selling advertising at the *Cambridge Evening News* ('The Voice of Mid-Anglia'), I was called to the lair of Carol, my sales manager, to undertake one of those initiative tests which unlock the secrets of your identity in about twenty minutes.

Carol was a woman for whom no statement was so direct that it couldn't be re-routed according to her own crazed logic. Among her oracles, she once advised me that 'When people say "no" to you on the phone, Andrew, what they really mean is "yes, but I have a few questions I'd like you to answer first".' This kind of watertight absurdity made her a lethally effective salesperson.

So, summoning the blood, I answered the questions as best I could and handed them to Carol, who, having pondered these things, informed me in a rather disappointed voice that I had turned out to be 'an amiable'. Not just 'amiable', you understand, but *an* amiable, as in *an* Eskimo. This revelation meant that, in her eyes, my sales career was as good as over – no great loss to their circulation as it turned out.

Yet the day had begun with limitless potential. When calling my clients on the Health and Beauty page, they might have heard my familiar, apologetic pitch (*So sorry to bother you, you probably won't want to do this, but would you like to …*) and thought that, hang on, a *New Year, New You* supplement could be a God-sent solution to their business needs. Or I might have changed my approach entirely; gone on the offensive like my power-selling colleagues, and demanded to know whether they realized the cost of missing out on such an unrepeatable opportunity: 'Turning this down could lose you a lot of potential custom – is that what you want? Well? Is it?'

But, twenty minutes in, I had been elected for damnation. I was an amiable: comforting and harmless, like a stuffed Koala.

The best personality tests aren't as straitjacketing as this. They give the individual some room for manoeuvre and view their responses as provisional – an indicator, not a definition, of character; opening up possibilities, rather than sealing them off. The worst sort, though, are maddeningly presumptuous. The only way to engage with the bally things is on their terms – you answer their questions and are categorized accordingly. No possibility is admitted that the questions may be inadequate or need qualifying; no opportunity is given to change or grow – no dialogue, in other words. It's enough to make you growl like a mastiff, even if your natural, amiable state is to grin like a half-wit.

You can tell it still smarts. Perhaps this is because summary judgement and dismissal of each other continues to be so damaging to the Christian Church. You can't help hoping that, somewhere in the mysteries of their CV, every bishop-elect has had a brief sojourn in telesales to prepare them for the wearying trial-by-ticklist they will face in the days ahead. All too often – in church and media culture – perfectly reasonable questions over specific issues become the dismissal of an entire ministry.

The approach is not unlike that of the Gileadites in the book of Judges, when they were trying to work out whether passers-by were their enemies, the Ephraimites. In the absence of their handily wearing a big 'E' on their tunics, they decided to ask them to pronounce the tricky noun 'shibboleth' (the equivalent, one assumes, of 'Worcestershire' in English). If they said 'sibboleth', their accent gave them away and they were (probably) first laughed at and then promptly put to the sword. It proved a devastating test and, we learn, a quick route to the grave for 42,000 men.

A besetting sin of the Church is that we regularly apply the shibboleth principle to those who are not our enemies, but our brothers and sisters in Christ. We badly need a sense of proportion which doesn't ignore the gravity of difference, nor even of error, but is able to work it through without immediately putting the knife in.

It seems that only history can give a sense of balance about the mixed bag our leaders are bound to be. Martin Luther famously suggested taking the Epistle of James out of the Bible because it didn't appear to fit his theology – neatly dismissing it as an 'epistle of straw'. Yet today, this outrageous proposal – set against the background of his achievements – is greeted with indulgent smiles of the 'ah well, that was Luther' sort.

It is no different when it comes to biblical characters: we rightly magnify King David for his faith, and view his murderous adultery as welcome evidence for roundness of character, with which to spice up our sermons. Likewise, we applaud the wisdom and poetry of his son Solomon, and overlook his 700 wives and 300 concubines as if he were a child taking more than his fair share of Maltesers.

The present reluctance to reflect upon the whole person is not limited to the Church of England, or the evangelical wing of it: a reductionist focus on 'issues' has come to lend a deadly pharisaism to all aspects of public life.

In this climate, two parables of Jesus which could well do with an airing liken the kingdom of heaven to a field containing both wheat and weeds, or a dragnet that catches all kinds of fish. The inference is that separating the righteous from the unrighteous is an extremely subtle business that has to be done carefully, at the right time and by the right person: Christ alone. Judgement is certainly coming, implies Jesus, but in the meantime we are to lay the scythes aside and grow together.

And the first person to mention the word 'amiable' can meet me outside.

28. Disorganized religion

By any standard, liturgy is an unappealing word. It sounds like a medical condition – some sort of involuntary spasm, perhaps, experienced by those under anaesthetic. *Any signs of liturgy in the patient, nurse?* Like its ugly sisters 'synod' and 'parson', it also has that damp, churchy quality that rarely lightens the mood when casually lobbed into conversation. All of which is unfortunate, given that liturgy is an inescapable feature of congregational life.

It derives from the equally unbeautiful Greek word *leitourgia*, meaning 'act of service' and appears in the Old Testament with reference to the work of priests and Levites in the temple. In the New Testament it crops up less frequently, applying more broadly to all acts of service, such as raising collections for the poor. In the early church, though, the meaning of liturgy gradually focused in on gathered worship – especially the Eucharist – and today it is generally taken to mean the structure or format of any church service.

Unsurprisingly, given what we know about the Church's genius for carrying its past along with it, the liturgy of both Eastern and Western churches displays a striking continuity over the centuries. In the unlikely event of a second-century Godfather like Justin Martyr popping today into an average parish communion, the chances are he wouldn't be entirely thrown by the proceedings. In a fascinating glimpse of early church life – little more than a century after the death of Christ – he records:

> And on the day which is called the Sun's Day there is an assembly of all who live in the towns or the country; and the memoirs of the apostles are read, as much as time permits. When the reader has finished the president gives a discourse … then we all rise together and offer our prayers: and … on the conclusion of our prayer, bread is brought and wine and water; and the president similarly offers up prayers and thanksgivings to the best of his power, and the people assent with *Amen*.

He goes on to mention the distribution of Eucharistic gifts, and even the collection: all that's missing are the notices.

More informal churches sometimes seem not to have a liturgy; and may assume that, because their prayers are off-the-cuff, they are automatically of-the-Spirit. But all worship has one, whether you are BCP or strictly OHP, and it pays to know where your service is heading. Organized religion, though widely condemned, is highly preferable to the disorganized version.

So liturgy is basically a good thing. Over the last century, what became known as the Liturgical Movement – also a patent cure for sciatica – has seen a wholesale rediscovery of ancient patterns of worship and the laudable attempt to renew modern services in their light. While this can yield record-shop snobbery (in the sense that the early stuff you've never heard is always the best), the movement has borne plenty of fruit, latterly in the introduction of the new Anglican prayer book, *Common Worship*.

This process of renewal has simmered away within the churches largely unbeknown to the rest of society, which explains both the dismay in the press about *Common Worship* and why this seems odd to anyone who has attended church on anything like a regular basis since the 1960s. Most of the latter are so used to liturgical revision that they wouldn't recognize the language of the Prayer Book if it reared up like an horse and smote them.

To the former, the new liturgy marks the apparent death of England's religious consensus: its common prayer. A much-loved tradition, tucked away in the nation's loft, has been remembered and, with one voice, the media reacted to *Common Worship* like an irate Parish Council and cried 'You can't touch that!'

Some of the criticism of the new services was so knee-jerk as to seem dislocated from that other endangered tradition, Common Sense, and a weary C of E might be forgiven for covering its ears and ploughing on regardless (if that isn't physically impossible).

But behind the whining there is genuine regret at the loss of wise old words, still ripe with meaning: and in the arrival of unfamiliar new ones, merely a confirmation that we are now farther from Eden than ever. Traditions – ancient or modern – are the way in which we gain access to faith; when they are altered or removed, we wonder where on earth God has gone. Truly to lose liturgy would be fatal for an age that already thinks it is left to its own spiritual devices.

As a rough primer, Anglican liturgy tends to be based around a call-and-response pattern, the reason for which may be easily demonstrated by watching an episode of under-fives TV favourite *Bob the Builder*:

Can we fix it?
Yes, we can.

It's fun, it's memorable and you can all do it together. That's liturgy.

Some of the new *Common Worship* prayers try a little too hard to be poetic and ends up just wordy. This can at least have some amusing results. Previously, intercessions would be punctuated with the simple:

Lord, in your mercy
Hear our prayer.

Easily done. However, now the intercessor will often announce to the congregation something like this:

'To the bidding:

"May the light of the glorious gospel shine ever on your pilgrim people, O Lord",

please respond with the words:

"And nourish us with the fruit of your empowering Spirit, so the Church might yield a harvest of righteousness."'

Not likely. What happens is that, caught unawares by the lengthy bidding, the keener members will try to pick up the response halfway through and say something like:

nurrwwirritarverr ... *sness.*

The alternative, however, is for 'liturgy lite', where the responses are breezier and more conversational – which soon stirs up any right-thinking congregation into an angry mob. To contain and defuse this, I have devised the following series of responses, which you are welcome, as ever, to insert in your Sunday service sheet.

Let all things that have breath praise the Lord!
Hallelujah!

Come now, I think you can do better than that. I said,
Let all things that have breath praise the Lord!
And we said hallelujah. Don't push it, sunshine.

Fair enough. Family well?
Quite well, all things considered.

That's the Spirit. Now, would you turn to your neighbour and tell them
your name?
We'd rather not, if it's all the same.

Please, turn to your neighbour, tell them your name and what you had
for breakfast.
If you keep this up, they will be able to see what I had for breakfast.

Point taken. Perhaps, then, you would like to split into small groups.
Perhaps not.

Come on, everyone, split into small groups of three or four.
**Unless *you* want to be split into a small group of three or four, I would
stop there.**

So then, as we join in worship together, let us dispense with sadness!
And also with you.

29. Enjoy God responsibly

Outside church for a few weeks has been parked a blue Vauxhall Astra, across the glove compartment of which the unknown owner has slapped a large sticker bearing the legend 'Relax! God is in control!' As I walk by I can't help but enjoy the image of the driver putting this advice into practice: reclining back and blithely careering down Gipsy Hill, feet folded on the dashboard, blind to the scattering panic.

Out of genuine concern for his welfare and that of other road-users I am preparing for him an even larger sticker, which reads: 'Concentrate! God has put you in control of this vehicle, and miraculously endowed you with all the complex faculties you need to drive it: if you don't use them you will surely die!'

By contrast, behind it is a black London taxi emblazoned with a huge advert for Jack Daniel's whiskey. Low on the rear wing is written, incongruously, 'Please enjoy Jack Daniel's responsibly'. Things really have changed: the very emblem of devil-may-care hedonism now wants me safely home by eleven. Keith Richards has become Mary Poppins.

Something in me recoils from this and wants to cry, 'No! Drink it rashly or wretchedly maybe; drink it vainly in Vegas from a silver stiletto, or vicariously in Stevenage from a Tesco tumbler; but whatever you do, don't drink Jack Daniel's responsibly. That's not what it's for. One might as well put such 'advice' on the side of an Exocet missile – 'Please annihilate others responsibly'. Perhaps they do.

Part of my reaction here is just old-fashioned harrumphing at the kind of overweening regulations which insist my butter wrapper carries 'allergy advice: contains milk'. Part again stems from that irksome sense of being done good to, made all the stronger by the assumption of a patronizing, nobody-enjoys-a-drink-more-than-I-do tone, which has as much clout as a foam hammer. The curtness of 'smoking kills' is infinitely preferable to this weaselling nonsense.

But I suppose the real problem is that, in different ways, the messages on both cars treat their readers like children. The first asks the driver to see themselves as a passenger in the back seat of life, with God at the wheel. All they need to do is let him steer and not interrupt. The second, whilst appearing to urge the opposite response, is similarly hand-holding: a kind of legislative lick wash.

As a paranoid parent whose sentences are punctuated by barked injunctions to caution (CAREFUL!! with that cotton wool / dangerously soft cushion etc.), I know how easy it is to view the world as one gigantic Health and Safety Nightmare. I also feel keenly the influence of what is popularly agreed to be the Rumsey family motto – 'Safer Not To' (whose heraldic devices include a raised drawbridge and three children, rampant). But it won't do, especially for those who believe in a creator God.

Because once you have come to view the world in this way, about the second thing which stares you in the face (after your own reflection, and the comedy of it being somehow divine) is the staggering, reckless risk involved in the creation project. The sense that anything could happen, probably will, and yet there being all to play for.

Whereas other ancient creation myths had the gods making the earth for their food – easy to swallow until you get to the indigestible bits, like Harlow – or as a disinterested spin-off from their wars in heaven, the Genesis account is focused, ecstatic and highly personal: it sounds like a peculiarly dangerous sort of fun.

Aside from the limitless potential for suffering and disaster, there is the strong possibility (proved correct after just two chapters) that humanity will opt not to return God's affection and, having been liberally showered with gifts like sex and summer fruits, might well choose to worship them instead. And that is just the start: long after the fall, the cliff-hanger continues.

Ethics is the study of how people may rub along well together in this kind of world, and is useful only insofar as it is realistic. Aristotle, assuming people's basic desire for a happy and fulfilled life, espoused what he called 'the golden mean': the midway point between extremities of behaviour, either of which is a vice. Courage, for example, between cowardice and foolhardiness. Upper Norwood, between the vicious extremes of Dulwich and Croydon.

Aristotle's ethics have been hugely influential, and are eminently sensible. Generally speaking, this balance is what most of us try to achieve. But I'm not convinced it's right. Nobody, pursuing the Golden Mean, would harness up the huskies and set off for the South Pole, for example, or spend their days wiping the flies off street children.

I accept that here I'm flying in the face of the Anglican *Via Media*, which tends to run a mile from extremism (or maybe half a mile – mustn't go too far). But 'moderation in all things' is a Roman proverb – from the suitably suburban-sounding playwright, Terence – and maybe not the best one for a Christian.

In the parable of the Prodigal Son, the fatted calf is awarded to the one who drank deeply and despairingly of the world and then, poor fool, tried to crawl back home. It is not given to the responsible, Aristotle-toting elder son. And it isn't fair. In the Parable of the Talents, things are even more extreme, with the cautious slave who buries his one talent being flung East of Eden, South of Norwood into Outer Darkness. Here, the message seems to be that life is a gamble – you can take the gamble or not, but if you don't, you'll die. Stick that on your Astra.

In these fables there is everything to gain – eternal life! And, inevitably, everything to lose. Disturbingly, the same pattern pertained in Jesus' real-life encounters: those who were keen to follow him, but who sensibly wished to settle a few domestic engagements first, or not keep all their eggs in one basket, were given short shrift. The faithful man or woman does not play safe, it seems.

Lent is time given to read the writing on the cars and decide how we are to live well behind the wheel. Fasting, abstinence and chastity – so often pitched as polar opposites to wild indulgence – are, in fact, very near neighbours. For with God, I'm afraid, it would seem to be all or nothing.

30. First name terms

Preparing to register my infant son's name, I've been toying with the idea of slipping in an extra one, just to broaden his palette of options. Naturally, we've chosen a biblical name for our newborn, but just in case little Tiglath-Pileser III runs into a bit of mild schoolboy ribbing for this, it might be wise to add in an alternative or two.

Happily, the family tree is bristling with worthy contenders, of which my clear favourite is Wyldbore – manful, dignified, and ever so slightly menacing. Nobody messes with a Wyldbore. But I suspect the Victorian surgeon originally bearing this elephant gun of a name would rarely have wielded it in public and it may be safely assumed that only his nearest and dearest would merit access to such nominal nether regions. The passing of an era when names and titles were a kind of body armour against incivility is captured in P. G. Wodehouse's penultimate Jeeves novel, written in 1971. When Bertie Wooster hears, to his horror, the blackguard Bingley addressing his valet as 'Reggie', there is a sense of the glory having departed. 'It had never occurred to me before that he had a first name', he reflects, disorientated.

The relentless informality that has ensued can occasionally prompt nostalgia for a time when to give another your Christian name was to admit them across the threshold into a privilege of closeness. I confess to feeling mildly affronted when any Tom, Dick or Harry (they didn't give their surnames), quoting me for car insurance over the phone, addresses me with the same name whispered in private by my wife. Wincingly unfashionable though they be, formalities and titles allow for appropriate levels of intimacy, offer the hallway before the bedroom. Once I have given you my name, I have nothing more to offer you – you have me.

It's an interesting point to consider in theology. When, transfixed by the burning bush, Moses is sent to Pharaoh, he asks, in effect, 'Whom shall I say called?' This was not his petrified approximation of an Egyptian Jeeves, but a penetrating question, for, to Israelites, a name revealed one's very essence. In Genesis, God had been known by various titles – God Most High, God Almighty and so on – which denoted aspects of his character. Here God uses for himself the enigmatic and awesome name I AM WHO I AM, usually translated in Hebrew as 'Yahweh' and, in English scriptures, as 'the LORD'.

You can almost hear Moses murmuring, 'Oh, ah … I see', for this stunning, sort-of-name both reveals and conceals, and hints at dimensions of being that the nervy little fellow clutching his sandals is never going to grasp.

Only when we have heard Moses' heart hammering at his ribs can we also hear the pin drop in John's Gospel when, centuries later, Jesus alludes to himself with this most sacred name, and begin to understand why the Pharisees picked up stones to stone him for blasphemy. Only then are we ready for the remarkable intimacy with God displayed by the one who invited his friends to address God as a toddler might address his dad. This is the 'Our Father' (neatly formalized by the English Bible following the Wodehousian *Pater* of the Greek translation) with which all Christian prayer begins.

In the Gospels, we are introduced to a Christ who appears not to stand on ceremony: an approachable Christ who invites himself home for tea, and calls the disciples his friends and family, 'because I have made known to you everything I have heard from my Father'. A Christ who, you feel, wouldn't be averse to felt-tipping his forename on a peely sticker should the occasion demand.

The implications of this behaviour sent the author of the Epistle to the Hebrews scurrying to his scrolls to revisit the language God's people had always used for intimacy with God – that of sacrificial worship – and write of now confidently 'drawing near' to God, entering 'the most holy place' and so on. Anyone could now be his entourage, his inner circle.

The journey from Yahweh to Christ Jesus is the story of a divine devotion that dares to speak its name. As such it involves an almighty risk of vulnerability, that the name given will be bandied or abused. When God gives us his name, he gives us himself, and we have him; we can etch it on our hearts or nail it to a cross.

It's a commonplace to hear that name dropped like litter by the careless; there is also the worrying way in which believers can presume an easy familiarity with God without also hallowing his name. When wayside pulpits announce the forename 'Jesus' in billion-point text I feel the same sense of slight violation, of a name unwittingly taken in vain. It may just be the Wyldbore in me showing his tusks, but I will still mutter 'That's *Lord* Jesus, if you don't mind', as I accelerate past.

In a curious and troubling twist to the Parable of the Wedding Banquet, which, *par excellence*, portrays God as the approachable host whose doors are thrown open to all-comers, Matthew's version mentions a guest who arrives at the palace improperly dressed, as if taking liberties with his free place at the table. 'Friend, how did you get in here without a wedding robe?' the king asks. Speechless, he is promptly bound hand and foot and thrown by the butlers out into the night.

31. Big enough for the both of us

The uncertain seconds between ringing someone's doorbell and their door opening have a peculiar suspense about them. One could still dash home (and a part of you always wants to), yet one is compelled to stay. Even when calling at a familiar address, the bell sounds an alarm both inside and out and you can never be entirely sure whether you will be greeted by warm grins or snarling terriers.

These threshold moments carry great imaginative power, which is why they often form the most memorable scenes in children's stories. Here, tension is heightened when the passage is between the everyday world and another, enchanted, state: fumbling through the fur coats in a wardrobe, or finding – as in *Where the Wild Things Are* – that your familiar bedroom is turning at dusk into a fantastic forest, creepers coiling around your bedposts. The rest of that book I can take or leave, but the image of Max's jungle room could hold me rapt for hours.

Sigmund Freud describes this transition as one between the *heimlich* (the 'homely') and the *unheimlich* (the 'unhomely' – usually translated as 'uncanny'). 'The uncanny', he writes, 'is that species of the frightening that goes back to what was once well known and had long been familiar', and 'often arises when the boundary between fantasy and reality is blurred'. Especially uncanny, suggests Freud, are situations which leave the reader wondering whether particular figures are real people or, in fact, automatons (insert your own joke about the PCC or General Synod here).

If so, then just about the most *unheimlich* moments of my childhood were spent listening to a scratchy 45 of the story *Sparky's Magic Piano*. In case you are fortunate enough to have escaped this experience, the plot concerns a small boy – Sparky – who is struggling to learn the piano, until, one day, the instrument comes to life. In a haunting musical voice it announces that it will play for Sparky – all he has to do is waft his hands convincingly over the keys. Thus enchanted, Sparky plays like a prodigy and astounds everyone, to the extent that he is booked to play a grand concert at the Carnegie Hall. Just as he raises his fingers to perform, the eerie piano speaks again, this time to inform Sparky that, with immediate effect, he will no longer play for him – thus leaving the hapless child transfixed before an audience of several hundred expectant adults.

So traumatized was I by this nightmare sonata that, despite repeated listens as a child, I can't recollect how the story ends. Sparky, as far as I'm concerned, is still stranded on that terrifying brink. Should any child of yours be displaying a precocious desire to perform, one spin of this tale should sort them out for life.

Our fears of the uncanny are surely a significant factor in the decisions we make about faith, whether as adults or children. 'Behold, I stand at the door and knock', says Christ in St John's profoundly disturbing visions in Revelation. 'If anyone hears my voice and opens the door, I will come into him, and dine with him, and he with me.' Despite the fact that we are the ones at home in this encounter, there are many who worry that inviting him in will soon find us cowering in the broom cupboard.

Growing up in a vicarage meant that God was, on one level, as homely as bathtime and Ronnie Barker. Yet I recall the keen sense of reticence and unease when, as a teenager, preachers would impress the need to 'let Jesus into my life', or for the Holy Spirit to 'take control' of me. *He must be Lord of everything*, they adjured, making the once familiar God sound uncannily like a bailiff come to repossess your house. This held me back from commitment for some time – thinking, not unreasonably, that the more there was of him, the less there was likely to be of me.

The fear that we will lose identity and freedom and become a radio-controlled Christian keeps many a door locked to the knocking man with the lamp. We want to be *ourselves*, not some sort of droid. The irony is that, when I finally did unchain the door to admit him (a decision I might have avoided indefinitely without such preaching), I found, paradoxically, that the more the Lord made himself at home, the more room there was for me. The cramped-looking police-box of faith turned out to be a TARDIS.

I had been concerned that the impact of the Holy Spirit (who, in Holy Ghost guise, easily appears as the most *unheimlich* member of the Trinity) upon me would be, at worst, that of the magic piano upon Sparky. At best, it might be similar to that described in the cartoon series 'Billy's Boots', from the boy's comic *Tiger*.

Billy was a lad who happened upon a pair of old football boots belonging to long-departed football ace, 'Dead Shot' Keen. Putting them on, he found that he was able to play just like his baggy-shorted hero. This was quite appealing for one who – on the football pitch at least – was less 'Dead Shot' Keen than

'Dead Loss' Rumsey. Yet, thrilling as the stories were, I was always left with the unsatisfactory sense that Billy, like Sparky, was something of a fraud and must have wondered who *he* really was and what he could achieve by his own merits – emotional subtleties which *Tiger* clearly didn't feel it was necessary to address.

Needless to say, neither of these scenarios applied when it came down to it. Accepting Christ probably won't automatically enable you to emulate your hero, nor will your feet or hands be guided as if by a divine puppeteer, only to be left dangling in mid-performance. Instead, it may feel more like a homecoming. And while the life of faith requires a constant and uneasy transition from one realm to another, unlike Billy, at least you can live with yourself.

32. The open door

It's not what you say that counts, but how you say it. This simple but vital life lesson is soon learned by people who have to say difficult things for a living, and I always admire those who deftly apply what is sometimes called the 'velvet fist' – the damning blow that is dealt with such smoothness and grace that those on the receiving end feel nothing but a sense of cowed gratitude.

With a certain pride I have observed that this is a gift peculiarly bestowed upon evangelical clergy. I remember the colleague who, presented in a staff meeting with a minor blunder by one of his team, responded, 'Could I encourage you never to do that again?' 'Encourage' is of course the key word here, for, as long as you do so encouragingly, you can say just about anything.

My favourite example features the incumbent of a certain West London church, who effortlessly sacked one of his staff with the words, 'We want to release you into all that God has in store.' You can imagine the poor sap shaking his vicar warmly by the hand, and wandering off down the high street beaming vacantly until he realizes he has just been done up like a Christmas turkey.

Which brings me to the purpose of all this – namely, to introduce your next guided meditation for the Lenten season, the success of which rests on the encouraging manner in which it is delivered. The main aim is to take a congregation of people on the kind of imaginary journey that allows them to see their everyday world afresh, as if they were a group of well-meaning aliens landing in Budgens. Feel free to dispense with this script if you feel an actual trip with them to Budgens will achieve a similar effect.

> Good evening … [*pause for a good 10 seconds here and ensure the lights are turned down ridiculously low*] and welcome to tonight's guided meditation for Lent. You may notice that it's become quite dark in here. That's because, theologically speaking, it makes things … feel sort of spiritual. Remember that, in Celtic spirituality, the dark represents … *the night time*, which is symbolized by a *great owl*. The *night owl*. In the dark, let us wait for the night owl to come …
>
> How do you think we should welcome him? You may wish to stay quiet, or, alternatively, you might like to make a noise like a tiny woodland

animal, remembering that owls are birds of prey and will always draw near when they hear a mouse, or a vole ... Squeak with me, if you like ... [*pause here to allow participants to squeak out loud – you may need to start them off*]. Is the night owl here yet? Let's wait a little longer ... [*soak up several minutes in this fashion if you've space to fill*].

What will you feel first when the night owl comes, do you wonder? His talons? His powerful beak? The ... insane flapping of his great wings? And how does that make you feel? Some of you might want to run away, which is understandable. But remember, the owl's eyesight is perfect – even in the dark – and he will find you.

And so, with the night owl having smothered us in his feathery blackness, I want you to picture yourself at a door – an *open door*. How saddening it is to find doors which are closed, locked up – existing only to keep others out. *Open* doors allow everyone in – they invite strangers into our home, free to come and go as they please, to help themselves to all that we have to offer. Are all your doors open tonight? I do hope so [*there may be some slight scuffling at this point as a few participants make their way outside to check their cars etc. – all quite natural*].

Tonight we are standing in the open door of a supermarket. Waiting, quite still, in the doorway, what is the first thing to catch your attention? Is it the busy murmur of conversation or the vibrant commerce? Is it, perhaps, the fact that you are blocking the entrance for others trying to come in? So often the world wants to carry us forward at its relentless pace, wants us to all walk the same way, never pausing to notice everything that surrounds us. But that is not our way – we live in God's time, and are called to stop and wait, however hard the world may find it.

When you are ready, and not before, just allow the pressure of bodies behind – all of whom have now discovered the meaning of waiting – to propel you into the shop, until you arrive at the dairy produce. Look around you: what a lot of margarine there is – a quite overwhelming variety of colour and size. Carefully, you might like to lift the lid of one of the tubs and slide your fingers inside, feeling its texture – bringing it to your face to smell, and maybe taste. If you like, gently smear some of the margarine around your cheeks and leave it there ... How strange that so few others are taking the time to do the same thing. What does it feel like to be so different?

You may wish to try this with some of the other produce that surrounds you in this place. In the quiet, I'm going to leave some space for you to choose which areas of the supermarket you want to discover [*it may be helpful to prompt people by mentioning a few aisles out loud – pickles and spreads ... wet fish ... and so on*].

And now, having touched and tasted all there is in store, you slowly move towards the exit. Regrettably, though perhaps inevitably, this is now a *closed door*, and you learn that Security has been called. Security. What a sad and empty word that is – for who or what can be secure when one is completely open? *In*security is surely what these poor people need – and what you can offer them, as they take you by the arm ...

33. Only a poor little sparrow

It may be the fault of The Ramblers. Not the ones with the Association, but the chart-topping juvenile choristers from the late 1970s. Around the same time that the infamous St Winifred's School Choir were sending every self-respecting grandma diving for cover with their unbidden affections, The Ramblers' equally cloying ditty 'I'm only a poor little sparrow' seems to have persuaded our feathered friends that it was high time they flew from the roost.

Whatever the grounds for its flight, the house sparrow is fast disappearing from Britain. While intensive farming has assisted its loss from rural areas, the decline of the sparrow in urban areas – a staggering 92 per cent since 1970 – is, according to the world's expert on *Passer domesticus*, Dr Denis Summers-Smith, 'one of the most remarkable wildlife mysteries of the last 50 years'. It has now virtually gone from our major towns and cities, prompting newspaper 'Save the Sparrow' campaigns, complete with hefty rewards for the first convincing explanation of its departure.

It may initially seem an unlikely cause for a crusade: after all, plenty of far more distinguished or indeed, attractive, species are also under threat in these times. A sparrow is, surely, just a sparrow. Which is precisely the point: the very fact that the cockney sparrer is the Ian Beale of the bird kingdom – the epitome of common-or-garden mundanity – is at the heart of its symbolic power, and consequently why its disappearance feels distinctly unsettling.

Added to which, it is, after all, the *house* sparrow, 'closely associated with man' as the *Hamlyn Guide to Birds* somewhat drily puts it. Rather more eloquently, the Book of Common Prayer makes the same point in its reading of Psalm 102: 'I have watched, and am even as it were a sparrow, that sitteth alone on a house top'. We have long been trained to see in the sparrow a parable of our own plight and if he can fall from his lofty perch, then, the inference is, so can we.

On one level then, the house sparrow is an icon of insignificance, as Bede observes in his eighth-century *Ecclesiastical History of the English People*. Our brief human lifespan is, he considers 'as if when on a winter's night you sit feasting with your eldermen and thanes, a single sparrow should fly swiftly into the hall, and coming in at one door, instantly fly out through another'. Yet it is an important sign of our Christian inheritance that what could prove to be a metaphorical counsel of despair, becomes instead a symbol of the small glories of life, its significant detail. In a nihilistic world, Shakespeare would never have let the 'special providence in the fall of a sparrow' slip from the lips of a morbid Hamlet.

Pivotal here has been our cultural digestion of Christ's own lessons in birdwatching, from St Matthew's Gospel: 'Are not two sparrows sold for a penny? Yet not one of them will fall to the ground without your Father's knowledge.' The simple virtue of being remarkably unremarkable has seen the humble sparrow become an icon of ordinary life inlaid with the suggestion of God. Because 'His eye is on the sparrow', runs the old Pentecostal hymn, 'I know that He watches me'.

As the sparrow's numbers plummet, scripture assures us that God sees – perhaps even wills – its descent from our skies. But possible divine judgements, like *Passer domesticus*, also tend to be closely associated with man, and recent evidence infers that it is our common garden habits that may be to blame. A report by German scientists into the sparrow's decline in Hamburg points to a similar fall-off in the numbers of greenfly upon which sparrow chicks depend for their first few days of life. Aphids may be the gardener's enemy, but they are mother's milk to such nestlings.

In which case, the unhomely truth may be that our love of pesticides has inadvertently also wiped out the bird that has always been our closest neighbour. What school choir would want their infants to sing such a murder ballad now?

34. Dynamo light

The lengthening of days, from which Lent takes its name, is a great release. Confined and tightly coiled by winter, we spring outside to reclaim the world like lost property. Here is the garden furniture, leached and grey, that I meant to take into the shed; there is the children's sandpit, shroud blown back under brickbats and pocked with fox dirt. Everything needs attention.

And, in the garage, bicycles. There is a strong attraction to cycling in spring, which is well worth the struggle to drag and dislodge my bike from the hose reel and all the clinging clutter flung in during chilly forays from the house. In terms of evocative smells (old paint tins, engine oil, cobwebs) garages rank alongside churches and, as such, are holy places, ideal for short retreats. They are time machines, where, as I fit the snaking adaptor through my spokes, I look up expecting to see my father's dark blue Raleigh, seat rigged impossibly high. Strapped beneath it was a canvas saddle-bag containing a puncture repair kit and two jingling clips, and, beneath that, was fixed a chrome dynamo light.

This, it must be said, was an unsatisfactory invention. I had one once and always enjoyed the soft growl of the dynamo as I pulled away from home – and the modest glow of pride at generating my own electricity. Pedalling along a flat road, the light would shine nicely, though it grew dimmer climbing a hill and became a sad amber ember by the time you reached the top. Its crucial flaw, however, became evident as soon as you had to stop at a junction. Then, at the very point when you most needed to be seen by other road users, the light would desert you, like the music of Sparky's Magic Piano. So you took your life into your hands (or feet, more precisely) and launched into the crossroads, hoping that the little reviving pulse of light would be sufficient to see you across.

Since those days, the dynamo lamp has seemed to me to be a metaphor for a certain kind of Christianity – the kind where everything is down to our own efforts. The hardworking hero of the God-helps-those-who-help-themselves brigade is, predictably enough, a Briton, named Pelagius, who lived in the fourth and fifth centuries AD. The teaching that bore his name, Pelagianism, viewed the fall of Adam essentially as a Poor Show – a bad example, which malingering humanity could learn from if they applied some discipline. By extension, the life and death of Christ became an extremely Good Show – a new ideal standard to which even the work-shy could aspire.

Creditable in its confidence in human nature, Pelagian faith just about guarantees failure, being the spiritual equivalent of the Stakhanovite rate of coal production introduced by Soviet Russia during the 1930s. This was based upon the Herculean efforts of Alexsei Stakhanov, who – by the blinding light of his helmet lamp – mined 102 tons of coal in one six-hour shift, fourteen times his quota. Mulling it over, the Stalinist authorities decided this would be a reasonable level to expect of every miner thereafter, and adjusted their production targets accordingly – which must have made Stakhanov popular in the colliery canteen.

Pelagianism, though roundly condemned by early church councils, has been remarkably persistent in Western Christianity. Consequently, plenty of believers roll along the road of faith feeling that, though the Lord may be present, the light falling upon their path relies on them to keep pedalling – the harder the better. So, naturally, when the road gets rough and steep, or a crossroads is reached, faith founders with the fading beam.

In his Gospel, St John seems at pains to say that this is not the case: that the light of life is generated by God's dynamism, not ours – by the power of glory. For John, glory is our one inexhaustible energy supply: an ancient and eternal current that anyone must connect to if they really want to live. It emanates from the relationship between Jesus and his heavenly father as a luminous blend of personality, presence and loving regard, circulated by the Holy Spirit.

In John's portrayal, this divine dynamo charges most powerfully at the points where human resources give out – when the wine runs dry at the wedding, or the well is deep and you don't have a bucket. Indeed, 'the hour for the Son of Man to be glorified' is the low-gear slog to the cross – a junction at which all other lights are extinguished. Just before the soldiers come ('with their lanterns') to arrest him in the garden, Jesus' last prayer asks the Father that his disciples may see for themselves the glory 'that I had in your presence before the world existed'.

Insofar as our role in this is active, it simply consists in the command to 'abide' in Christ: to remain connected to him like components in an electronic circuit. Even our ability to do this is securely earth-bonded by the Holy Spirit, promised to Jesus' followers just before his death. Glory is thus something given to us; something that, writes St Paul, we all reflect to one degree or another – some of us swathed in luminous vests, others relying on the small red disc on our rear mudguard.

Back in the garage, my bike is unfettered and ready to ride, while outside, even the lengthened day has given way to darkness. Yet, freewheeling into the failing light, the night is lit with glory.

35. Sanctimonious drivel

By far the most enjoyable thing to issue from a more strident secularism in public life has been the enthusiastic airing of some of the most delicious and condescending put-downs the mother tongue has to offer.

Listening recently to the phone-in after *Any Questions* on BBC Radio, which had featured some calmly non-flammable comments from the Archbishop of Canterbury, in whizzed a call bemoaning Dr Williams' 'moralistic hand-wringing'. Chances to employ 'hand-wringing' with any real vigour ideally require a senior churchman on the receiving end in order to convey the right sense of clammy-palmed paranoia about moral issues. Slip in 'the good bishop' before your criticism (as in 'I'm sure the good bishop means well ...') and the game is as good as over.

There is no point denying it: the Church invites the best insults. These, like all the finest abuse, usually come double-barrelled and are extremely satisfying to say: 'sanctimonious drivel' pretty much takes the prize here, rolling round the tongue like wine before being disdainfully spat out. Its close cousin, the neatly dismissive 'pious claptrap' is fairly irresistible, too. If you find yourself held in church against your will, there are few more cathartic things to do than mutter 'sanctimonious drivel' darkly under your breath during the sermon. Only make sure your mike is turned down.

Happily, you see, God-botherers can also use such fiery darts to lob at our over-inflated brethren. Indeed, whilst Christians have their own armoury against the world ('filthy heathen' still sounds rather good, for instance), they have tended to reserve their sniffiest epithets for fellow believers of a different ecclesial hue. My late aunt, a nun, used to relish telling how my great-great grandfather, an Anglo-catholic parish priest, had once been requested to take a funeral for the local Baptist minister, who was on holiday. 'Would you bury a Baptist?' they enquired, politely. 'I'd gladly bury the lot of them,' came the disparaging reply. Touché, old ancestor.

Insults generally aim to make an opponent's position appear fatuous or eccentric, while simultaneously painting one's own stance as the acme of objective good sense. Very often, then, they have far more to do with us than those we are criticizing, shoving another into the wings in order to stand in the spotlight ourselves. The best ones, however, are not quite so calculated and spring from moral outrage on another's behalf.

Jesus' own terms of abuse are interesting here. He did have some belters, usually aimed in-house at the Pharisees, that 'brood of vipers', whom he readily labelled 'whitewashed tombs' and 'blind guides'. This invective erupts most dramatically in the Gospel passage known as 'the six woes'. Jesus, we learn, has been invited back to a Pharisee's house for a meal. Before they've even served the soup, the latter observes that the Lord hasn't washed his hands properly before the meal. This clearly touches a raw nerve, and Jesus proceeds to rain down a hailstorm of sarcastic abuse on these 'unmarked graves' who sit round the table.

After three woes – denouncing the Pharisees' vanity and neglect for the poor – his flabbergasted host says, limply, 'Teacher, when you say these things, you insult us.' Get away. Jesus – who is just warming to his theme – ignores him entirely and piles on another three woes for good measure. 'Woe to you, "experts in the law",' he sneers, 'because you load people down with burdens they can hardly carry, and you yourselves will not lift one finger to help them.' And then – scripture doesn't record the 'Pah!' – he walks out. *Salad, anyone?*

Given his evident loathing for all the Pharisees stood for, Jesus' choice ultimately to yield to them is all the more arresting. When the temple guard came for him in the garden, the logical climax of their feud was Peter's ear-slicing sword, not the lamb-like submission. The way Christ silently soaks up insults is focal to the ensuing story of his Passion – the gormless mockery of the soldiers, the braying crowd, and, finally, the not-very-good joke hammered over his comedy crown. With the public cheering him on, and everything to fight for, the Nazareth firebrand suddenly allows himself to be stamped out, deliberately losing the argument.

Now, as Quakers and queers have found, there is something genuinely disarming about taking a decent insult and wearing it proudly. But the cross of Christ is something far rarer, and related to how St Paul explains the wrath of God – that is, not in terms of smiting the offender but (far more chilling, this) 'giving them over' to what they want. Letting people see the logical end of their action, without divine prevention. As such, Christ's triumph on the cross is a martial art, letting the enemy overreach and exhaust himself, allowing the full force of the offensive to become the means of its own downfall.

Insults, well crafted or otherwise, have limited range. Whilst they keep the derided viewpoint at arm's length, crucially they don't make it disappear. And although full-throated ridicule of all that is wicked and vain is vital to any good fight, it never really wins, partly because it's what you are for that enables victory, not simply what you oppose.

The problem for Christianity's cultured despisers in our own time is that much of what the atheists are for – scientific method, for example – most Christians are not against, and much of what they are against – religious violence, say – most Christians are not for. Christianity – let alone religion as a whole – is such a huge target, sprawling across centuries and cultures, that you can't help but hit it. Infuriatingly for those who have it in their sights, it is also so big that you can't help but miss it, like an elder brother who just yells 'didn't hit me' every time you finger-shoot him at point-blank range.

Dry your hands, then, peddlers of pious claptrap, for you know you can take it.

36. Letting it fall

Clergy are wonderfully useless in times of crisis. With precious little to offer save a knack for empathy, we mysteriously appear at emergency scenes like superheroes bereft of special powers. We don't, as a rule, pursue the fleeing villain over the rooftops, nor do we hold up the creaking viaduct or quell the rising flood. Yet beside the striped barrier tape or bleeping life support, the clergy may be found, renewing their acquaintance with grief, trying not to get in the way.

The fact that we aren't responsible for actually *doing* anything at such incidents is precisely why, on occasion, the coped crusader can be indispensable. But not always. Just recently, I was strolling past the off licence, as two delivery men were unloading a pallet piled six feet high with cases of wine and corseted with shrink wrap. They'd managed to haul the pallet trolley off the pavement and onto the road, but the load had been badly stacked and was listing precariously. As it began to topple, they hurried round, trying to embrace it upright, like a glassy-eyed companion.

Sensing the call to assist, I sped over to offer a reassuring presence or to see if anyone needed a pastoral chat. It seemed not, so I joined them in their doomed attempt to hold up the leaning tower of Pinot Noir. Several others gamely did the same, though we all got glued in the same dilemma, where we couldn't push the straining boxes back but, equally, daren't let them go. So we simply stood there, wheezing, in what you would have to call an impasse.

Presently, a passer-by sidled up and, with the wisdom of experience, said, 'Lads, it's not going to work – you've just got to let it fall.' He was right, of course. However reluctant we were to admit it, our tipsy cargo needed to collapse. So, on the count of three, we dived out of the way, while the bottles, sensing their moment had come, tumbled and shattered, spilling the wine like blood into the gutter.

In the Gospels, Jesus appears to have taken a similar view of the teetering burden of religious law supported by faithful Jews. Try as they might to live a righteous life, they were trapped, one way or another, by its cumbersome demands. This is what St Paul – who, as a former Pharisee, was in a position to know – called a 'yoke of slavery', and he despaired of ever being able to carry it. 'I can will what is right', he wrote to the Romans with disarming frankness, 'but I can't do it.'

For Jesus, the whole problem focused on the temple in Jerusalem, the massive, towering edifice of organized religion that he and the disciples wander around in the days before his arrest. Galilean tourists, they gaze up in awe at the portico and one of them says 'Look teacher, what large stones and what large buildings!' To which Jesus, like a wise builder, sucks in the air over his teeth and responds (in so many words), 'It's no good, lads, this whole lot's going to have to come down.'

Around the same time, he prophesied that he would raise the temple up again within three days of this unavoidable destruction. Given that Herod's Temple covered an area four times the size of Windsor Castle, and had taken 46 years to build, this must have seemed improbable, even to his friends.

But such was Jesus' popular support by the time he reached Jerusalem that it was a claim taken with deadly seriousness by the chief priests. Not because he would literally take a wrecking ball to the temple (though he displayed his inclination to do so by driving out the moneychangers) but because he taught a new sort of faith that bypassed its regulations altogether: one based around allegiance to himself. This 'easy yoke' that he offered to all who laboured and were heavy laden was what made him so threatening and, ultimately, intolerable to the religious authorities. He was making them redundant.

As the gospel story reaches its climax, Jesus appears to make the decision to bear in his person the whole penalty of the religious law – as if to pull down the temple around himself, like Samson amidst the Philistines. He clearly saw this as the way in which a new kind of law – a new testament – would be inaugurated, whereby his followers might be freed from the impossible trap of knowing how they ought to live, but never being strong enough to manage it: spiders in a bathtub, forever slipping back down.

Jesus would make his own body the means of escape – he would become like a hopeless sinner and soak up the desperate consequences, so that his 'little flock' would never have to again. Henceforth, faith would be defined by simple allegiance to him and the heart of the old covenant – love of God and love of neighbour. Everything else, you suspect, might need to collapse.

Lent is the time when we recognize our uselessness in the face of sin, our inability to hold up the hazardous burden of righteousness. The time when we take the advice of the wise passer-by, who says, 'Come on, lads, it's not going to work: you've got to let it fall. You go. Let it fall on me.'

37. Race most wondrous

Standing alone, haloed by the first flies of spring, the silence of a graveyard is overwhelming. The dead don't seem absent, just quiet – dumbstruck in the face of glory. To feel the hush at the end of our babbling is an invaluable Lenten lesson, and only emphasized by the epitaphs mouthing mutely from each headstone. In various states of decay, these protruding teeth carry poignant reminders of how words eventually fail us.

One such example is in the churchyard at Crickhowell in Powys, where rest several generations of my family. Here, an inscription commemorates my forebear Walter Rumsey, who died in 1834. Under his name, is engraved a quote from the Psalms: *Mark the perfect man and behold the upright, for the end of that man is peace.* Trusting that this was a sentiment volunteered by his family and not Walter himself, you read on: *Also of Anne, relict of the said Walter Rumsey … 'She hath done what she could'.*

At first view, this glaring contrast with her stainless spouse looks like a rather unkind slight, a sort of glossed-over version of 'poor dear'. That is, until you notice that it, too, is a direct quote from scripture, being Jesus' words of rebuke to the dinner guests who moan about the woman pouring the jar of costly perfume over his head. 'Let her alone', he growls. 'She has done what she could; she has anointed my body beforehand for its burial', adding that her action will live on in memory wherever the good news is proclaimed.

Suddenly Anne, relict of Walter, emerges from the shadows: not as a paragon, perhaps, but as someone who did what she could. Someone who, given their lease of life and aware of its constraints, invested each opportunity with devoted, even extravagant, attention. The more you think about it, the finer an epitaph it becomes. After all, much of the time I don't do what I can: I avoid the possible task by pondering on what I would do if things were different. This kind of wishful thinking robs us of the potential to find what Paul Tillich called 'the eternal now' – the immense significance of the present moment. Ultimately, it is ignorant both of life and death, a daydream of immortality. Doing what we can, on the other hand, anoints the body for its burial.

The satisfaction of Anne's tribute makes a refreshing change, given the restlessness conveyed by many others. Gravestones sit like a classroom of transfixed children waiting to be picked, each slab a raised and rigid hand. This is particularly evident in the memorial masonry of middle-class Victorians, who were eager to invest death with the same elaborate self-importance as they were apt to display in life.

Another windfall from the family tree shows this with wincing clarity. It is – using the term as generously as possible – a poem, composed 150 years ago by my great-great grandfather, Revd John Williams Rumsey, and entitled, with Christlike humility, 'Race most wondrous':

Race most wondrous among races,
Grand depot of gifts and graces!
Who can ever number rightly
All the charms ye shew so brightly?
Clearest eye can only some see
Of the virtues of a Rumsey.

Quick in body, quick in mind;
Wise, yet bold; profound, yet kind:
Lion hearts most staunchly true,

> Deeds of gentle love to do:
> Strong in art, in word, in pen:
> Prophets, leaders among men.
>
> But o'er all your powers is found
> One by which the whole is crowned.
> Strange to tell, more strange to find
> (Race to your own merits blind),
> *Modesty* most wondrous strong
> Checks you as you go along.

If only it had. Sparing you the remainder, I think we may conclude that Victorians of this stamp were not greatly encumbered with a sense of irony.

My excuse for exhuming this appalling slice of self-deluding doggerel is that it shows how hard genteel Britons strove to establish that they were *someone*. 'Pedigree' was a vital part of this exercise, serving to bolster one's place in society. Indeed, you still hear this or that aristocratic surname absurdly referred to as 'one of the oldest families in England' as if all families weren't equally old. Victorian genealogy was self-consciously aspirational, and strained the branches to breaking point for a touch of quality. It is, then, no surprise to find the same generation that penned 'Race most wondrous' also managing to carve out a family tree whose tenuous twigs linked us – via family pets and vague acquaintances – to Alfred the Great and the Emperor Charlemagne.

Israel's messiah had to have the right breeding – to be born of David's line. While incidental to us, knowing who begat whom was crucial for the framers of scripture, for they were telling the story of a single family, called by God to be a light unto the nations. These people knew their roots, so when Matthew wrote a gospel for the Jews, he suitably started with the block from which the carpenter's son was chipped. Matthew's genealogy, however, was a radical departure, mainly because it included women. Women, moreover, with the whiff of scandal clinging to their memory – like Tamar, who posed as a prostitute in order to get impregnated by her father-in-law. Or Rahab, the harlot who did what she could.

A common ancestry in Adam and Eve confers nobility and notoriety on us all, and makes our blustering epitaphs seem charming, perhaps, but quite redundant. The teacher will choose us when we have quietened down. So, in the graveyard, our fly-blown haloes are best worn in silence.

38. Reality Checkpoint

Parker's Piece, Cambridge

Trapped behind the high walls of a Sunday pew, with little for a boy to do but watch his hassock swing hypnotically on its hook, a palm cross once a year made lavish entertainment. Far better than the poppy we got on Remembrance Day (the black popper and petals of which could be removed, but that was all), the palm cross was a kind of liturgical Transformer.

Principally, it was a sword to fight with, whose hilt was just the right height for a small fist. For non-combatants, it was also a craft project, which could be slowly unfolded into a single spindle then carefully pieced back together. The especially mischievous, however, could tear its fibrous ridges into little strips and shreds. And not pick them up. If, by some slim chance, your cross survived Palm Sunday, it might be pinned to a notice-board, abandoned in a drawer, or magnetized to the fridge.

The cross crops up everywhere: sheer profusion throughout life is the basis of its pulling power. 'Think for a moment, and ask yourself if the business of the world could be carried on without the figure of the cross', observed the second-century apologist Justin Martyr, in the earliest known study of Christian symbolism. 'The sea cannot be crossed unless this sign of victory – the mast – remains unharmed. Without it there is no ploughing; neither diggers nor mechanics can do their work without tools of this shape ...'

This makes it hard to see the rood for the trees, for unlike its great semiotic rival, the circle, the cross is the scaffolding of the world. It marks intersection – which, from Tudor beams to tube maps, is the essential frame and support of society. Its colossal strength holds opposite forces in tension and whereas the circle suggests completeness and harmony, the cross bears irreconcilable difference.

To cap it all, cruciform is the definitive human shape: *Homo erectus* with arms outstretched – a fact which can provoke Pagan complaints of Christians stealing it from everyman. Given its natural employment as the Church's brand identity, this is understandable. Yet despite clip-arted appearances as the logo for your local fellowship, scripture affirms that the cross doesn't belong to us, it belongs to the world. When the Son of Man is lifted up, Jesus said, he will draw all people to himself. The Church is simply the community of those who have recognized their self-portrait and whose confession follows accordingly: 'we are the body of Christ'.

Because it can never be a registered trademark, the 'religious' threads cannot easily be unpicked from the cross-stitch. Indeed, hallowing the cross only intensifies its pulling power on popular imagination, such that it can repel a Vincent Price vampire and still be as attractive as a lover's kiss; can be both the red cross of relief and healing and the fearful plague-tag daubed on a door.

Such contrasts only brighten its appeal as a fashion accessory. Whether diamond-encrusted by Christian Lacroix or – at the other end of the chain – grimly pierced by cadaverous Goths, the cross is still an image to die for. But although the darkness may not have understood it, the cross is always at home to paradox, especially on 'the Calvary that is our signpost', as R. S. Thomas describes it, with 'arms pointing in opposite directions to bring us in the end to the same place'.

In the city of Cambridge, there is a flat mat of parkland called Parker's Piece, where townsfolk wipe their feet before entering the university's domain. Here, in the middle of its criss-crossing pathways, stands an ornate cast-iron lamppost, affectionately known since the 1970s as Reality Checkpoint. No one knows quite how it came to bear this inscription, apart from a likely origin in the midnight ramblings of inebriated students, glad of a reassuring landmark as they stumbled home through the fenland mist. Despite periodic attempts by the city council to erase the legend, happily Reality Checkpoint is always re-christened, its name currently scratched in with a compass.

In a similar way, those who have erred and strayed return to the old rugged cross in order to take their bearings and plot their course. Because x marks the spot, believers naturally want to ring-fence their reality checkpoint and prevent a careless public carving other graffiti into its trunk. But their Lord takes the matter out of control – now, as then.

Raising his palms, Jesus surrenders himself to being handled by fools; fought over, stripped, pinned down and abandoned. And in leaving the world free to decide what to make of him – to weigh him in the balance – the cross finally resembles nothing so much as a pair of scales. Which, one way or another, does justice to us all.

39. Scarecrow

Outside the Salvation Army citadel, a generously built man of about fifty summers is jumping on the spot, clapping enthusiastically to a mufti brass band. He is wearing, or has grown, furry rabbit ears and is bellowing hearty greetings to startled passers-by, all but manhandling them into the hall for the Spring Fayre. This is the Saturday before Easter, and the Church is taking to the streets.

Nobody can scare crows like Christians do and this is the week to prove it. Hot-crossed preachers blunderbuss the Good News to swerving shoppers; beach donkeys clop ropily down suburban closes; crucifers lead billowing choirs past Primark. 'This is Holy Week' the catholic placards proclaim, reminding me of the window sign in a Cambridge furniture store that declared, proudly, 'This shop is 200 feet long!' Nice to know, I always felt, but it didn't especially draw me in.

These banners capture the perplexing nature of what are generally called Acts of Witness, which aren't demonstrations in any normal sense. Come Good Friday, we shall be gathered on the grass outside Sainsbury's. There will be a cross, a bath sponge on a bamboo cane and a crown made of brambles. We will read excerpts from the passion story through a microphone, drowned out by the lawnmowing din of its own generator. We will have a stall giving away cold buns and a wodge of service leaflets, paperweighted by a tub of Flora. It may well rain. We're not protesting against anything, neither are we calling for anything to change. We are just there, witnessing, and I will be inordinately proud to be present.

Like most believers, I have experienced the full spectrum of emotional response to busking the gospel, from fearless keenness to acute and searing embarrassment. As a young Christian I leapt at every chance I could find to give my faith an airing, including one memorable trip to a 'March for Jesus' in London (he hadn't requested one, as far as I could tell, but what the heck). On the train from Reading, amphetamined with the spirit and insulated by numbers, we began to rehearse some of the songs we expected to sing on the impending non-demo. I'm truly sorry if you happened to be one of the passengers that day: it must have been excruciating – and of course you had no viable means of escape, bar the emergency cord. But at least we were entirely safe, which could be less confidently said of the equally boisterous band of Scottish football fans, heading to Wembley and singing just as lustily at the other end of the carriage.

It didn't take them long to notice they were not alone in their pre-match euphoria, and, inevitably, a kind of choral competition arose between us, to the mute dismay of the commuters sandwiched in-between. It could have all got rather hairy, but, instead of a fight (which, it seems fair to assume, we would have lost instantly), what ensued was a good-natured truce on the Great Western Front. They joined us at our end and soon swore allegiance – we supping their McEwan's: they sharing our bags of Quavers. Then, in the general mood of cooperation, one of our new friends suggested, beerily, 'I tell you what – you sing one of our songs and we'll sing one of yours.'

The risk that their riper lyrics might prove a stumbling block was far outweighed by this unparalleled opportunity for an Act of Witness. So we did – and I shall never forget the sound of a dozen tanked-up Scots, cans swaying aloft, chanting 'Mek way! Mek way! For the KENG OF KENGS', as we spilled out onto the platform at Paddington and embraced each other like brothers.

In the intervening years, this readiness to make public displays of affection for God subsided markedly, such that I will still turn on my heel and walk in the opposite direction when hearing the megaphone blast of a street evangelist. But whether you present it coolly or cackhandedly, the gospel of Christ has an inescapable magnetism to it, which will repel as many as it attracts. 'To the one we are a fragrance from death to death', writes St Paul to the Christians in Corinth, 'to the other a fragrance from life to life. Who is sufficient for these things?' This is the unresolved tension at the heart of a faith that seeks to reach the whole world, yet accepts that most people will give it a wide berth.

The cross is meant to be offensive, after all, and cannot be toned down, no matter how well the Church sands and stains it. Calvary is a place of impossible choices and it cannot accommodate everyone. In fact, when you get to it, there is only one it can accommodate, for all others have fallen away. Worst of all, it is unavoidably public, this stark stick, pricking up through history. The cross is the splinter of the world, and it tugs at our flesh most uncomfortably.

Therefore, if we feel its pull, there must be a time to be foolishly obtrusive about our faith: when we lay self-consciousness aside and stand out like a sore thumb. It makes perfect sense for that time to be Good Friday, when human folly is paraded so blatantly.

On that day, a group of church members will wander around our parish with a rough cross: silently for the main part, but stopping at points to tell the story and sing a hymn or two. One of these, near the railway, is a station where all the contradictory forces of our neighbourhood seem to converge. It, like the small bevy of believers who muster there, is a peculiar mix of white and black, posh and poor, and we meet with our song-sheets flapping where the junkies score and professionals pour out up the hill. Here might we stay and sing, inviting ridicule. For no holier place exists, and nobody there would be anywhere else.

40. Live in extraordinary beauty

Riding in hearses is a singular experience. The sense of suspended reality it affords is partly due to slow motion, wheezing along at a stately 15 miles per hour whilst the traffic tapeworms behind you. Also it has to do with other people's response, many of whom stop to cross themselves as you pass – something that only rarely happens to me when on foot – and their always allowing for you, letting you through, moving at your pace. It's a little like being in *The Truman Show*.

Just recently, my limousine had inexplicably broken from the pack somewhere around South London's heart of drabness, Thornton Heath, and arrived at the cemetery with several minutes spare for the driver and myself to get to know each other a little better. As we stood stiffly by the graveside, he leant over and, in the conspiratorial tone beloved of undertakers, remarked, 'I don't know whether you've noticed this, sir, but if you look closely around the cemetery, you'll observe that all the headstones face towards Croydon.' 'It's quite deliberate,' he added, just to hit the nail home.

Gawping about like a halibut, I realized to my astonishment that he was quite correct. Taking myself in hand, I recovered sufficiently to counter that, if my friend were to look even closer, he might detect the residents ever so slowly turning back the other way. Nevertheless, his remark had left a deep impression: the thought of so many prone souls gazing for all eternity, not on the heavenly Jerusalem, but on the pedestrianized purgatory of the Whitgift Shopping Centre was fairly discomposing.

This memorable episode reinforced the truth that mortality is the basis of all humour. That and funny jokes, of course. In his book *Wishful Thinking*, The American novelist Frederick Buechner contends that both are also closely related to faith. As evidence he spotlights the Bible passage where God tells Abraham and his geriatric wife, Sarah, that they are about to have a child, at which news the old man keels over in hysterics, 'falling on his face' with merriment, according to Genesis 17. Meanwhile God keeps up the fun by telling them they are to name the boy Isaac, which, in Hebrew, means *laughter*. 'Faith', concludes Buechner, 'is laughter at the promise of a child called laughter.'

Comedy lies in the gap between what we could be and what we are. Comic timing depends on eternity being set into the heart of men and women, and those mortals knowing the absurd shortfall. Bathos – the lapse from sublime to ridiculous – is thus the comedian's stock-in-trade.

In scripture, this familiar routine is shaken up in the person of Jesus, whose resurrection rewrites the ancient joke about the bloke who's alive, but then dies. The timing seems to be all over the place, but, for those who get it, the punch-line makes sense of everything else.

The divine comedy thus lies in its climax rather than its content. Whilst there is no shortage of wit in Jesus' teaching, the Gospels are rarely funny in an explicit sense. Jesus wept, but did he laugh? G. K. Chesterton thought that the Messiah's mirth was the one great quality he kept hidden from the world, wondering if it erupted when he stole up the mountains to pray. But I suspect that it was not Jesus who hid his humour so much as the Gospel writers, for whom it might not have been on their biographical agenda.

In adversity, laughter and tears can almost be simultaneous; both coming out in hard bursts, like tap water under pressure. Given this, it is quite possible that a desperate mirth may have intensified alongside Christ's grief in the days before his trial. I imagine the Lord's laughter exploding across the table at the Last Supper, perhaps even bleeding out with the sweat in Gethsemane: hosanna in extremis.

During the passion narrative, though, the only humour is sick mockery, targeted at an unprovoked Christ. Reflecting on it after the event, St Paul seems to see the time when Jesus deadpans his detractors and takes their sentence on himself as the key moment in a dark and deeply ironic comedy. 'We preach Christ crucified', he writes to the Corinthians: 'unto the Jews a stumbling-block, and unto the Greeks, foolishness.' The very point at which weary slapstick is flogged to death – where nothing is funny any more – this is where an entirely new act is taking shape. 'Because the foolishness of God is wiser than men', Paul observes, dryly, 'and the weakness of God is stronger than men.'

Somewhere in that shrouded silence between Friday night and Sunday morning, the last laugh breaks out. Easter Day reveals wholly original material, which challenges us to revisit all that is clapped-out and predictable. To see Christ in our place, and imagine how that place might be resurrected.

Those who really glimpse this are sometimes, like comedians, depressive and slightly unhinged, as was the case with South London visionary, William Blake. Blake's most balanced and clear-headed act seems to have been attempting to persuade his father at the age of ten that he had seen hosts of angels in a tree at his local park, Peckham Rye (to which his father doubtless responded, *Don't be ridiculous, boy, there are no trees on Peckham Rye*).

His epic poem, 'Jerusalem', is a cracked and fantastic picture of England infused by paradise, of earthly and heavenly cities overlapping. Calling the country to awake from her 'sleep of death', he cries:

> And now the time returns again:
> Our souls exult, and London's towers
> Receive the Lamb of God to dwell
> In England's green and pleasant bowers.

Heading back from the cemetery through Thornton Heath, funeral over, there is an orphaned roundabout, blankly stared at by careless scraps of housing. On this desert island, moated by motorists, there have appeared hoardings heralding an unlikely new development to be built right in the middle. With unintentional hilarity the billboards fanfare the new homes with the legend: 'Live in extraordinary beauty'.

You can't fault them for trying: the sign could have been put there by Blake himself. And it shows that a slow car to Croydon is just the thing to bring to an end Lent's pregnant pause and graveside grin, as we cling to the promise of Isaac. Abraham got the joke, and it was counted to him as faith.

Acknowledgements

A number of the chapters in *Strangely Warmed* first appeared in my column of the same name on the website 'Ship of Fools'. My thanks, therefore, to the editor of that well-tuned organ, Simon Jenkins, for his encouragement and vision, and to Jeremy Begbie for his initial recommendation. Likewise, one or two cropped up in *Third Way* magazine, and I'm grateful to Simon Jones and Huw Spanner for inviting my contributions.

Thanks are also due to those whose good conversation led to some of these thoughts taking shape: to Mark Brend, Andy Griffiths, Malcom Guite, David Perry and Robert Titley for wit and wisdom; to Mark Stafford for reading through the manuscript – and the story about the rucksack; to Andy Green for the one about the airshow; and to Keith at West Norwood Cemetery for the brilliant tale about the coffins in the Thames. The Vicar of Crickhowell, Barry Letson, was most helpful, as has been my colleague Mary Bowden, whose tireless assistance freed me up to complete this volume.

My gratitude extends in particular to the parish and people of Christ Church, Gipsy Hill, who have forborne my ministry with admirable resilience over the past nine years. They, and the place itself, have been an inspiration.

Thank you to Caroline Chartres at Continuum and, lastly, to my lovely wife Rebecca, to whom this book is dedicated.

Photograph credits

Bishop Howes (p. 10)

Church Times

Jesus grafitti on Brighton West Pier,
by snub23 & orticanoodles (p. 13)

Photo by Martin Poole

'Please empty "*the urn*" after use' (p. 29)

Photo by David Perry

William Walker (p. 39)

The Historical Diving Society

Close neighbours in Old Kent Road,
London SE1 (p. 42)

Photo by Jim Harris

'He did it for you' (p. 53)

Photo by Simon Jenkins

Jesus Nut from a Bell helicopter (p. 71)

Photo by Alan Radecki/
Mojave West Media Works

Abandoned shopfront in Thornton
Heath, Croydon (p. 74)

Photo by Martin Salter

'Parker's Piece, Cambridge' (p. 107)

Photo by Sean Crawford

Andrew Rumsey is Vicar of Gipsy Hill in South London. He is married to Rebecca, with three young children.